THE LAND
&
THE GARDEN

V. Sackville-West

THE LAND & THE GARDEN

A new edition illustrated by
Peter Firmin
with an introduction by
Nigel Nicolson

Webb & Bower
MICHAEL JOSEPH

First published in this edition in Great Britain 1989 by
Webb & Bower (Publishers) Limited
9 Colleton Crescent, Exeter, Devon EX2 4BY
in association with Michael Joseph Limited
27 Wright's Lane, London W8 5TZ
Penguin Books Ltd, Registered Offices: Harmondsworth, Middlesex,
England
Viking Penguin Inc, 40 West 23rd Street, New York, New
York 10010, USA
Penguin Books Australia Ltd, Ringwood, Victoria, Australia
Penguin Books Canada Ltd, 2801 John Street, Markham,
Ontario, Canada L3R 1DA
Penguin Books (NZ) Ltd, 182–190 Wairau Road, Auckland 10,
New Zealand

Designed by Peter Wrigley

Production by Nick Facer/Rob Kendrew

The illustrations were engraved on vinyl
and reproduced from original prints. The
text is set in 12/14 point Plantin

British Library Cataloguing in Publication Data

Sackville-West, V. (Vita), 1892–1962
The land; & The garden.
I. Title
821′.912

ISBN 0–86350–272–5

Typeset in Great Britain by Keyspools Limited,
Golborne, Lancashire.

Printed and bound in Great Britain by
Butler & Tanner Ltd, Frome and London

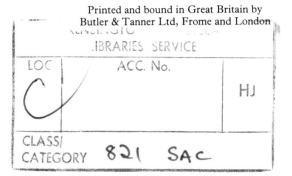

CONTENTS

DEDICATION

NIGEL HOLLIS
PUBLISHER
1943—1988

The publishers of this book dedicate
it to the memory of Nigel Hollis who
conceived the idea of an illustrated
edition and whose initiative made it
possible.

INTRODUCTION

Vita Sackville-West hoped above all to be remembered as a poet. She thought her novels *The Edwardians* and *All Passion Spent* too facile to deserve the acclaim they attracted, and would have despaired that today she should be known mainly as a gardener and a prose writer about gardens, much as she loved her own. She considered *The Land* and *The Garden* (the latter she rated second in quality, but wrongly) as her claim to an enduring place in literature.

The Land was frequently reprinted after its first appearance in 1926, but *The Garden*, which she published twenty years later, has been almost forgotten. In this edition they are re-issued for the first time in a single volume, as she would have welcomed, for they are complementary.

Vita was not a 'modern' poet. She once confessed to her husband, Harold Nicolson, that her poetic gears would not mesh with Eliot's or Auden's: 'It is something left out of my make-up . . . I mean just lack of interest in what must always be *temporary* things', like politics or ephemeral experiences, which modern poets, she believed, often expressed in language unintelligible to the ordinary reader. Her two major poems deal in part with the humdrum occupations of farm and garden, but her theme is universal, evoking the rhythm of the four seasons as they repeat themselves endlessly like the heavenly bodies circling above—she was fascinated by astronomy—and impose a pattern on the lives of those who work on and with the soil.

Vita stated as precisely as she could the subtleties of what she observed and thought. Her meaning is immediately clear, and discloses to the reader what he would probably never put into words himself but recognises as true, like 'Water alone remains untouched by snow', which everyone knows, but how few notice. She took immense pains with her writing: both poems, each about 2,500 lines long, needed years to complete and polish. *The Land*, first conceived in 1921, was begun in 1923 and finished in 1926, and she started *The Garden* early in 1939 and finished it late in 1945, overlapping the Second War at each end. Her successive drafts, now in the Huntington Library, California, reveal how she would return again and again to a line or single word that displeased her, until she found the phrase which fitted the metre and expressed her intention exactly: 'Little sullen moons of mistletoe', or 'Brings him achievement with the truce of age'. There is a homely felicity in the rhythm of her lines. She varied the blank verse which she normally used by breaking from time to time into rhymed couplets, and sometimes lyrics (she used italics, too, to give them emphasis), where she became more playful or more reflective, as in her lovely lines on fritillaries or the 'Island' passage, the most famous in *The Land*, which anticipates *The Garden* by its eulogy of the flowers she loved most. Her poetry has a sobriety, a balance, a gentleness and unfaltering taste. It is old fashioned, though nobody complained of that, in the deep tradition of English nature poetry. These lines, for instance, about sheep in winter,

> With looks of dumb despair, then sad-dispersed,
> Dig for the withered herb through heaps of snow

could have been written by Vita Sackville-West. In fact they come from Thomson's *The Seasons*, written exactly two centuries before. I think she was influenced by him, not by Virgil's *Georgics* as was commonly supposed, for she knew no Latin and did not read them in translation until she was halfway through *The Land*.

Vita was determined not to sentimentalize the countryman or his unending combat with the soil. Nobody has felt more profoundly the beauty of her Kentish landscape, but her purpose was to explain the alternating conflict and collaboration between man and nature which created it, and her wonder that something so lovely as a garden or a field of corn could emerge from so much muck, toil, wastage and mutual malevolence. She looked Nature straight in the eye, reacting against the romanticism and prettiness of nineteenth-century poets and painters, and found the land spiteful. Her labourers are peasants, little removed from serfs, their lives brutal and their manners loutish, taciturn and grave. They are not people, like Hardy's rustics, so much as symbolic figures in a landscape, yet there is a dignity about their labour because it is harsh, honest, anonymous and shaped, like their tools, by centuries of experience. So much nobler, she thought, than townsmen's lives, who

> Meet together, talk, and grow most wise,
> But they have lost, in losing solitude,
> Something, —an inward grace, the seeing eyes,
> The power of being alone.

Some critics felt that Vita had drawn too stark, too anachronistic, a picture. Where were the farmworkers' moments of joy, of companionship and love, the pub, the Church, the festivals and the cricket field? Why does she mention women and children so seldom? Why cast such scorn upon social change, or the encroaching means of lightening their daily work—the tractor, the baler and the car? There are no benign middlemen in *The Land*, no shopkeeper, no parson and no squire. Life is terribly basic. Winter, because it is the cruellest season, is counted the most typical, and the vagrant, dying in the snow, its symbol. Even her own farmland is denied its fecundity: 'Only a bold man ploughs the Weald for corn', she asserts of land which, before me as I write these words, is green with burgeoning wheat, and the garden behind me spangled with her flowers.

But Vita was resolved to pare her poem to the bone, to rid it of all soppiness, to restore to her countryside its medieval primitiveness and virtue by a salutary douche of pain. She introduces words of archaic origin, like undern, lusk, shrammel, winsel, boggart, yeavy, shippon; phrases like 'Eild sheep, wethers, hoggs and barren yoes', or, 'That mobled blossom and that wimpled tree', not to tease the reader, but to bring him up short by an obsolete, Jabberwocky word, to roughen the line, to suggest Anglo-Saxon or Chaucerian roots, and if it is not always intelligible nor to be found in any dictionary, the sense can be guessed from its onomatopoeic sound or deduced from the context, as if reading a foreign language with which one is not perfectly familiar.

There is another element in *The Land* which is rarely repeated in *The Garden*: its detailed instructions on how to govern the soil. Vita was not herself a farmer, but she owned a farm close to Long Barn, her house in the Weald of Kent, and let it to Vera Cardinal, whom she often visited and watched at work. Some of her most apt descriptions, like her clipped sheep which 'Staggers astonished from such curt release', or horses, 'Their shining shoes strike fire on errant flints', emerged from her close observation. Season by season she went down to the farm to watch a particular process and then return home to turn it into words. I often accompanied her on such trips and, though she did not take notes, I would see her go straight to her study and tell me she was not to be disturbed. I was eight years old at the time.

Thus she moulded her didactic passages—how to build a hayrick, how to tend bees, reap corn, dry hops—supplementing her own observations by reference to a four-volume Encyclopaedia of Agriculture which Harold gave her, and farmers said they could not fault her. The swarming detail has a cumulative effect. The poem must be long to permit its full development, to suggest the slow turning of the seasons with their interpenetrating tasks and moods, and to contrast the mortality of man with self-renewing nature, a theme to which she returned with increasing anguish in *The Garden*.

She finished *The Land* in Persia, and dated it at the end, 'Isfahan, April 1926', which led some people to imagine that it was all written there. In fact, at Isfahan she added only the last twenty-four lines in proof, her invocation of Virgil whom she at last recognised as her progenitor:

O Mantuan! that sang the bees and vines,
The tillage and the flocks.

It is her most sublime passage, lifting her homesick love of England from the deepest wells of her memory. She was pleased with it, but many years later, in her own copy, she altered the penultimate line from 'Thou took'st the waxen tablets in thy hand' to 'You took the waxen tablets in your hand', thinking the first version too emollient and wishing to end her poem as austerely as she had begun.

The Land was awarded the Hawthornden Prize, and John Drinkwater, in presenting it to her, said that the poem contained some of the loveliest verse written in this century. Most critics endorsed his praise: only Edith Sitwell voiced strong objections, calling it 'poetry in gumboots', which would 'be of great use to prospective farmers, for it is one long catalogue of agricultural implements'. She cannot have read it. Virginia Woolf, who was always Vita's frankest critic, encouraged her to write another long poem, about a village. Vita began it immediately, but it was not about a village: it was *The Garden*. She told Harold, 'It will have much more in it than mere gardening—all my beliefs and unbeliefs'.

Vita put *The Garden* aside for many years while she was writing her best-known novels, then *Saint Joan of Arc*, *Pepita* and *The Eagle and the Dove*, and took it up again in February 1939, working on it intermittently throughout the war, of which she had a more direct experience than most of her countrywomen. Her two sons were serving in Africa and Italy, and her house, now Sissinghurst, lay immediately below the air-battles of 1940 and close to the front line of the expected German invasion. Once, a huge bomber, crashing in flames, missed her tower by a few feet. She was courageous and defiant, her innate conservatism matching her profound patriotism, and she found beauty in the grimmest manifestations of war, like the searchlights,

> Slow scissors walking up and down the black,
> Soundless collision of their closing blades,

or a bird struck dead by a bomb falling in her own fields, on which she wrote one of her loveliest lyrics, 'It took a ton of iron to kill this lark'.

To her, the garden was a luxury in war ('Small pleasures must correct great tragedies'), and though it was perforce neglected and its lawns became hayfields, her plants continued to blossom unaware of the human crisis. Vita had a fellow-feeling for her flowers. For her they had almost personal characteristics, exuberance and sulkiness, arrogance and modesty, and she never lost her astonishment that something so short-lived, with no middle-age between bud and death, could put itself to so much trouble to look so beautiful. Her long passage about tulips is one example, and another, on daffodils and narcissus, expresses her amazement that a blade so tender and flexible could thrust its way upwards with such determination. Nature does most, she insisted, the gardener least.

Vita describes in detail how to cut hedges or to pot and prune, but now her purpose is more meditative, *The Garden* a profounder poem than *The Land*. The notes she addressed to herself on the margins of her manuscript reveal her main concerns: 'Courage in adversity: Determination to find pleasure and not succumb'; 'Dislike of modern life and vulgarity; love of the graces of life and retirement'. She felt a spiritual weariness, regretted her advancing age (though she was only forty-eight in 1940), remembered with a sigh the daring of her youth, and foresaw the end of life, rising in despair to capital letters:

ONE HOUR WILL BE THE HOUR OF DEATH . . .
IT IS ALREADY LATER THAN YOU THINK.

Vita was not formally religious, but she had pondered deeply, when writing *The Eagle and the Dove*, on religion's mysteries, and wished herself more receptive to its consolations. Her mood was sombre, her meditations suffused with melancholy, from which she aroused herself by examining the perfection of a flower.

On the day before publication in 1946 she hid herself in a wood 'from sheer misery' as she wrote in her diary, 'failing as gardener, failing as poet', as she wrote in the poem itself. She need not have worried. *The Garden* was widely acclaimed and won another prize, the Heinemann. Now, after an interval of many years, it is republished with its more lauded companion, and the two poems can stand together as the testimony of a writer who won from the soil the tribute she gave it.

Nigel Nicolson
Sissinghurst Castle
Kent

THE
LAND

WINTER

I SING THE CYCLE of my country's year,
I sing the tillage, and the reaping sing,
Classic monotony, that modes and wars
Leave undisturbed, unbettered, for their best
Was born immediate, of expediency.
The sickle sought no art; the axe, the share
Draped no superfluous beauty round their steel;
The scythe desired no music for her stroke,
Her stroke sufficed in music, as her blade
Laid low the swathes; the scythesmen swept, nor cared
What crop had ripened, whether oats in Greece
Or oats in Kent; the shepherd on the ridge
Like his Boeotian forebear kept his flocks,
And still their outlines on our tenderer sky
Simple and classic rear their grave design
As once at Thebes, as once in Lombardy.

I sing once more
The mild continuous epic of the soil,
Haysel and harvest, tilth and husbandry;
I tell of marl and dung, and of the means
That break the unkindly spirit of the clay;
I tell the things I know, the things I knew

Before I knew them, immemorially;
And as the fieldsman of unhurrying tread
Trudges with steady and unchanging gait,
Being born to clays that in the winter hold,
So my pedestrian measure gravely plods,
Telling a loutish life. I have refused
The easier uses of made poetry,
But no small ploy disdain to chronicle,
And (like that pious yeoman laid to rest
Beneath the legend that told all his life
In five hard words: "He tilled the soil well")
Prune my ambition to the lowly prayer
That I may drive the furrow of my tale
Straight, through the lives and dignities I know.

Why should a poet pray thus? poets scorn
The boundaried love of country, being free
Of winds, and alien lands, and distances,
Vagabonds of the compass, wayfarers,
Pilgrims of thought, the tongues of Pentecost
Their privilege, and in their peddler's pack
The curious treasures of their stock in-trade,
Bossy and singular, the heritage
Of poetry and science, polished bright,
Thin with the rubbing of too many hands:
Myth, glamour, hazard, fables dim as age,
Faith, doubt, perplexity, grief, hope, despair,
Wings, and great waters, and Promethean fire,
Man's hand to clasp and Helen's mouth to kiss.
Why then in little meadows hedge about
A poet's pasture? shed a poet's cloak
For fustian? cede a birthright, thus to map
So small a corner of so great a world?

The country habit has me by the heart,
For he's bewitched forever who has seen,
Not with his eyes but with his vision, Spring
Flow down the woods and stipple leaves with sun,
As each man knows the life that fits him best,
The shape it makes in his soul, the tune, the tone,

And after ranging on a tentative flight
Stoops like the merlin to the constant lure.
The country habit has me by the heart.
I never hear the sheep-bells in the fold,
Nor see the ungainly heron rise and flap
Over the marsh, nor hear the asprous corn
Clash, as the reapers set the sheaves in shocks
(That like a tented army dream away
The night beneath the moon in silvered fields),
Nor watch the stubborn team of horse and man
Graven upon the skyline, nor regain
The sign-posts on the roads towards my home
Bearing familiar names—without a strong
Leaping of recognition; only here
Lies peace after uneasy truancy;
Here meet and marry many harmonies,
—All harmonies being ultimately one,—
Small mirroring majestic; for as earth
Rolls on her journey, so her little fields
Ripen or sleep, and the necessities
Of seasons match the planetary law.
So truly stride between the earth and heaven
Sowers of grain; so truly in the spring
Earth's orbit swings both blood and sap to rhythm,
And infinite and humble are at one;
So the brown hedger, through the evening lanes
Homeward returning, sees above the ricks,
Sickle in hand, the sickle in the sky.

Shepherds and stars are quiet with the hills.
There is a bond between the men who go
From youth about the business of the earth,

The earth they serve, their cradle and their grave;
Stars with the seasons alter; only he
Who wakeful follows the pricked revolving sky,
Turns concordant with the earth while others sleep;
To him the dawn is punctual; to him
The quarters of the year no empty name.
A loutish life, but in the midst of dark
Cut to a gash of beauty, as when the hawk
Bears upwards in its talons the striking snake,
High, and yet higher, till those two hang close,
Sculptural on the blue, together twined,
Exalted, deathly, silent, and alone.

And since to live men labour, only knowing
Life's little lantern between dark and dark,
The fieldsman in his grave humility
Goes about his centennial concerns,
Bread for his race and fodder for his kine,
Mating, and breeding, since he only knows
The life he sees, how it may best endure,
(But on his Sabbath pacifies his God,
Blindly, though storm may wreck his urgent crops,)
And sees no beauty in his horny life,
With closer wisdom than soft poets use.
But I, like him, who strive
Closely with earth, and know her grudging mind,
Will sing no songs of bounty, for I see
Only the battle between man and earth,
The sweat, the weariness, the care, the balk;
See earth the slave and tyrant, mutinous,
Turning upon her tyrant and her slave,
Yielding reluctantly her fruits, to none
But most peremptory wooers.
Wherever waste eludes man's vigilance,
There spring the weeds and darnels; where he treads
Through woods a tangle nets and trips his steps;
His hands alone force fruitfulness and tilth;
Strange lovers, man and earth! their love and hate
Braided in mutual need; and of their strife
A tired contentment born.

I then, who as a wrestler wrought with earth,
Bending some stubborn acres to my will,
Know that no miracle shall come to pass
Informing man, no whisper from Demeter,—
Miraculous strength, initiated lore.
Nothing but toil shall serve him; in their rote
The seasons shall compel his constancy,
(The fields not always fair, nor prospects kind,)
Year ripen year, and timely foresight yield
Its measure in due course. And so I sing
Without illusion, seeing fieldsmen go
Heads lowered against sleet, hands frozen red,
Without complaint, but only patient, patient:
So in December sing I, while they come
Weary and dull and silent, tramping home
Through rainy dark, the cowman taking down
The hurricane lantern from its usual peg,
And going round the cattle in the stalls,
The shifting, munching cattle in the dark
And aromatic stalls beneath the rafters,
Swinging the lantern as he goes his rounds,
Clapping the kine upon their bony rumps
And seeing to their comfort ere he comes
Back to the ruddy kitchen for his food,
—Thus sing in winter, watching by the fire:

Many have sung the summer's songs,   *Winter*
Many have sung the corn,   *Song*
Many have sung white blossom too
That stars the naked thorn—
That stars the black and naked thorn
Against the chalky blue.

But I, crouched up beside the hearth,
Will sing the red and gray;
Red going-down of sun behind
Clubbed woods of winter's day;
Of winter's short and hodden day
That seals the sober hind:

Seals him sagacious through the year

19

Winter
Song

Since winter comes again:
Since harvest's but another toil
And sorrow through the grain
Mounts up, through swathes of ripest grain
The sorrow of the soil.

No lightness is there at their heart,
No joy in country folk;
Only a patience slow and grave
Beneath their labour's yoke,—
Beneath the earth's compelling yoke
That only serves its slave,

Since countryman forever holds
The winter's memory,
When he, before the planets' fires
Have faded from the sky,
From black, resplendent winter sky
Must go about his byres;

And whether to the reaper's whirr
That scythes the falling crops,
He travels round the widening wake
Between the corn and copse,
The stubble wake 'twixt corn and copse
Where gleaners ply the rake,

Or whether in his granary loft
He pours the winnowed sacks,
Or whether in his yard he routs
The vermin from the stacks,
The vermin from the staddled stacks
With staves and stones and shouts,

Still, still through all the molten eves
Whether he reaps or hones,
Or counts the guerdon of his sweat,
Still to his inward bones,
His ancient, sage, sardonic bones,
The winter haunts him yet.

Winter and toil reward him still
While he his course shall go

According to his proven worth,   *Winter*
Until his faith shall know   *Song*
The ultimate justice, and the slow
Compassion of the earth.

Hear first of the country that shall claim my theme,   *Andreds-*
The Weald of Kent, once forest, and to-day   *weald*
Meadow and orchard, garden of fruit and hops,
A green, wet country on a bed of clay,
From Edenbridge to Appledore and Lympne
Drained by the Medway and the Rother stream,
With forest oaks still hearty in the copse,
Sylva Anderida to Romans. Here
Stretched Andredsweald, and joined the wood of Blean,
Forest and warren, cropped by herds of deer,
And droves of swine that stirred the oak-trees' mast,
So wild a tract, so darkly green,
No stranger might forsake the trodden way,
Or venture through the trees towards the dene,
But on his horn must blow a warning blast;
No stranger, under Ina's law, might burn the tree,
And send the flame to sear the leaf;
If so he did, he must pay grudgingly
The fullest fine, for fire's a silent thief;
But if he took an axe to fell the oak,
Even several oaks, as many as might be
Then must he pay for three, not more than three,
For axe is an informer, not a thief,
And at the felling loud in protest spoke.

This was the Weald, compact of forest laws,
Pannage and Gavelswine, Danger and Corredy;
Unhandseled, separate, dark;
Where herdsman, seeking through the sunless days
For berry and for nut,
Shaggy with skins and hung with scarlet haws,
While hogs between the trees went grunting ways,
Lived a brute's life with brutes, and scored the bark
To blaze the track that led him to his hut
This was the Weald, but as man conquers slow

Andreds-
Weald

Each province of his fief,—poor simple land
Or ravelled knowledge,—so the tardy herd,
Waking to action, by impatience stirred,
Bethought him he might throw
Trees round his hovel, clearings make by hand,
And in the sunlight let his children go.

So grew the dene.
Next came the wooden plough,
Turning the furrows of the first bold field,
A patch of light, a square of paler green,
Cupped in the darkness of the Weald.
Hedges fenced off the boar, the bundling sow
Followed by squealing litter; hedges made
By loppings of the bough,
With teinage rudely thrust between.

Thus the foundations of the farm were laid.

The Weald
of Kent

The common saying goes, that on the hill
A man may lie in bed to work his farm,
Propping his elbows on his window-sill
To watch his harvest growing like a charm.
But the man who works the wet and weeping soil
Down in the Weald, must marl and delve and till
His three-horse land, fearing nor sweat nor droil.
For through the winter he must fight the flood,
The clay, that yellow enemy, that rots
His land, sucks at his horses' hooves
So that his waggon plunges in the mud,
And horses strain, but waggon never moves;
Delays his plough, and holds his spud
With yeavy spite in trenching garden-plots,
The catchy clay, that does its utmost harm,
And comes into his house, to spoil
Even his dwelling, creeps into his bones
Before their time, and makes them ache,
Leaving its token in his husky tones;
And all through summer he must see the clay
Harden as brick, and bake,

And open cracks to swallow up his arm,   *The Weald*
Where neither harrow, hoe, nor rake   *of Kent*
Can rasp a tilth, but young and eager shoots
Pierce into blank, and wither at the roots.
Yet with his stupid loyalty he will say,
Being a wealden man of wealden land,
Holding his wealden honour as a pledge,
"In times of drought those farms up on the ridge,
Light soil, half sand,
With the first summer gale blow half away,"
And lifts his eye towards the hill with scorn.

But only a bold man ploughs the Weald for corn,
Most are content with fruit or pasture, knowing
Too well both drought and winter's heavy going;
So the lush Weald to-day
Lies green in distance, and the horizon's sweep
Deepens to blue in woods, with pointed spire
Pricking the foreground by the village tiles,
And the hop-kiln's whitened chimney stares between
Paler and darker green of Kentish miles,
And rarely a patch of corn in metal fire
Burnished by sunset ruffles in the green;
But meadow, shaw, and orchard keep
The glaucous country like a hilly sea
Pure in its monotone. Sad eyes that tire
Of dangerous landscape, sadder minds
That search impossible regions of their quest,
Find clement haven after truancy,
A temperate answer, and a makeshift rest.
This is the thing familiar, known;
The safety that the wanderer finds
Out of the world, one thing his own.
A pause, a lull in journeying, return
After the querying and astonishment;
Reward that only rovers earn
Who have strayed, departed from the peace,
Whether in soul or body widely flown,
Gone after Arabian Nights, the Golden Fleece,
And come back empty-handed, as they went.

Winter   Hear next of winter, when the florid summer,
            The bright barbarian scarfed in a swathe of flowers,
            The corn a golden ear-ring on her cheek,
            Has left our north to winter's finer etching,
            To raw-boned winter, when the sun
            Slinks in a narrow and a furtive arc,
            Red as the harvest moon, from east to west,
            And the swans go home at dusk to the leaden lake
            Dark in the plains of snow.
            Water alone remains untouched by snow.

            Here is no colour, here but form and structure,
            The bones of trees, the magpie bark of birches,
            Apse of trees and tracery of network,
            Fields of snow and tranquil trees in snow
            Through veils of twilight, northern, still, and sad,
            Waiting for night, and for the moon
            Riding the sky and turning snow to beauty,
            Pale in herself as winter's very genius,
            Casting the shadows delicate of trees,
            Moon-shadows on the moon-lit snow, the ghost
            Of shadows, veering with the moving moon,
            Faint as the markings on the silver coin
            Risen in heaven,—shades of barren ranges,
            Craters, and lunar Apennines, and plains
            Old as the earth, and cold as space, and empty,
            Whence Earth appears a planet far surpassing
            Our ken of any star for neighbouring splendour,
            Her continents, her seas, her mountain ranges
            Splendid and visible, majestic planet
            Sweeping through space, and bearing in her train
            Her silver satellite that sees no strife,
            No warring of her men, no grief, no anger,
            No blood spilt red to stain the golden planet,
            But sees her architecture royally:
            Dark Asia; islands; spread of the Pacific,
            The silver satellite that casts the ghost
            Of ghostly trees across the fields of snow.

            Now in the radiant night no men are stirring:

The little houses sleep with shuttered panes;   *Winter*
Only the hares are wakeful, loosely loping
Along the hedges with their easy gait,
And big loose ears, and pad-prints crossing snow;
The ricks and trees stand silent in the moon,
Loaded with snow, and tiny drifts from branches
Slip to the ground in woods with sliding sigh.
Private the woods, enjoying a secret beauty.

But one man comes, one outcast and a vagrant   *Vagrant*
Having no roof to keep him from the snow;
Comes with a shuffling step between the trees;
Vague, old; and sinks upon a fallen bole,
Merging himself in night till silence gains him,
And hares play fearless round him in the shadows
Cast by the moon. Whence comes he? what have been
His annals? what but annals of long roads,
All roads alike, made sharp by hostile eyes,
—Rightly, he yields it, in his resignation,—
Whence has he shambled, into snow-bound Kent?
Out of what night of lassitude and despair
Into this night of beauty and cold death?
What sire begot, what mother cradled him?
He drowses on his bole, while snow-flakes gather,

Vagrant While snow-flakes drift and gather,
Touching his darkness with their white, until
He grows to an idol in the wood forgotten,
Image of what men were, to silence frozen,
Image of contemplation and enigma,
So stiffens in his death. His old coat covers
His heart's vain hieroglyph. But still the hares
Play hopscotch with the shadows, having less fear
Of death's quiescence than of life's quick danger,
In a world where men are truant, night to dawn,
Suspended hours when life's poor common business
Lies dormant in a world to silence given,
Given to silence and the slanting moon.

Shepherd Only the shepherd watching by his flock
Sees the moon wax and wane; endures the time
When frost is sharpest; hears the steeple chime
Each hour neglected; hears the rutting brock
Scream in the night; the prowling dog-fox bark;
Snared rabbit cry, small tragedy of dark.

The shepherd watching by his ewes and theaves
All night in loneliness, each cry knows well,
Whether the early lambing on the Downs
Rob him of Christmas, or on slopes of fell
March keep him crouching, shawled against the sleet;
But there's a cry that drowns
All else to shepherd's ears: the wavering bleat
Of weakling newly-born: then he shall lift
The lanky baby to his own warm hut,
Lay it on straw, and shift
Closer the lamp, and set the bottle's teat
With good warm milk between the lips half-shut,
Coaxing the doubtful life, while wind and rain
Against the window of the cabin beat,
And homing cottars in the plain below
Look up, and seeing the window's yellow glow,
Mutter, "The shepherd's at his job again."

Poor heavy-sided ewes must have their care;

Pasture, and in their pens a bite of hay.
Poor roots, good lambs; good roots, poor lambs, they say;
So shall the prudent shepherd keep them spare,
And likewise short of cake before they ean;
And he shall set the double hurdles square
Against the north and east with straw between,
For shelter; he shall run his ewes and lambs
In various pens: the twins, the little rams,
And frolic younglings just about to wean;
He shall turn little rams to little tegs,
And dock their tails, but on a different day;
Then, well content, sit down to watch them play,
Companioned by his pipe and towsled pup;
Watch them, appraising strong and frisky legs,
And grin when little ewe butts little tup.

But while the shepherd lonely in his cotes   *Yeoman*
Lives the harsh months decreed,
The farmer, thwarted by the early dusk,
Uses the hours that keep his ploughman lusk,
And plans his year for pasture or for seed.
Champion and several each claim their meed;
Fallow, and arable, and clover ley;
Shall the Ten-Acre carry sheep or oats?
Shall the poor Roughets stand this year for hay?

For now when fields beneath the wintry light
Lie stark, and snow along the hedgerow clings,
When streams of rooks on swerving wings
Blacken the sky with their untidy flight,
When the iron ridges bind the frozen clay,
And sunset reddens cart-ruts on the road,—
Now in the wolf-month, shrammed and gaunt,
When vixens prowl, and hopping birds grow bold,
And craven otters haunt
The coops, by famine driven, and by cold,—
There's little chance for labour on the land.
Only the dung-cart with its reasty load
Creaks safe across the fields on frozen ground,
And horses for the fork or shovel stand

Yeoman Patient, their nostrils smoking on the air.
Carting's a winter job. The strawy mound,
The wedge-shaped hale of roots for winter feeding stored,
Gapes, and gives up its rolling, orange hoard,
Cut in the farmyard troughs to equal share.
There's little else in these dead months to keep
The farm-folks brisk; at dawn and dusk they go
To break the ice on inky water-holes;
Fold on fresh patch of swedes the fattening sheep;
Put in a casual hour to dig out moles.
All desultory tasks, while the short day
Dulls from the morning's red to undern grey,
And dyes to red again as sun sinks low.

Then pencil in hand beneath the hanging lamp
The farmer ponders in the kitchen's hush;
In the dark shippon tranquil cattle crush
Sweet cake, sliced mangold; shift, and blow, and champ;
In the dark stable tired horses stamp,
And nuzzle at the manger for their feed.
But though the homesteads in such stillness doze
Under the double spell of night and frost,
Within the yeoman's kitchen scheme
The year revolves its immemorial prose.
He reckons labour, reckons too the cost;
Mates up his beasts, and sees his calf-run teem;
Takes pigs to market underneath a net;
Sees blossom on his orchards in the spring;
Sees rows of roots, all plump and stoutly set,
And hears the windy barley hiss
Like golden snakes before good harvesting;
And, since no little winsel comes amiss,
Cozens the dullards that go marketing.

He'd cheat a fool indeed, but do no worse;
His heart is wider than his purse,
Take all in all; but narrower than each
The portals of his speech.
Few words must serve his turn,
For he's sagacious who lives taciturn,

And airs no noisy cunning of his trade,   *Yeoman*
But keeps his private purpose deeply laid;
Gives neighbours nothing of his confidence,
And takes his counsel of his own good sense.
No wise man utters what he inly knows;
Certainty in a loose uncertain world
Is far too firm a treasure; wiseman goes
Jealous and wary, keeping darkly furled
His small particular knowledge. So he plots
To get the better of his lands again;
Compels, coerces, sets in trim, allots,
Renews the old campaign.
His mind is but the map of his estate,
No broader than his acres, fenced and bound
Within the little England of his ground,
Squared neat between the hedgerows of his brain,
With here Lord's Meadow tilted on a hill,
And Scallops' Coppice ending in a gate,
And here the Eden passing by a mill,
And there the barn with thatch,
And here a patch of gorse, and there a patch
Of iris on the fringes of a pond,
And here Brook Orchard banded safe with grease;
All this he sees, and nothing sees beyond
The limits and the fealty of his lease.
Tenant of his inheritance,
Brief link in life's long circumstance,
One of the nameless, name-forgotten line
Descended from that nameless ancestor
Who cut a holding in the serried weald
Where droves of swine
Rootled for acorns underneath the oaks,
Anderida's sole yield
When Drake played bowls at Plymouth, and the rare
Coach with the cumbrous spokes
Trundled along the single clay-wet track
To Sussex with drawn blinds, or journeyed back
To London on affairs of state, the fine
Heraldic blazon eloquent on the door;
Makers of land, one of the nameless line

Yeoman That fenced, and tilled, and overcame the waste,
And cut the necessary gaps,
And shaped the fields, slow-paced,
Into their permanent design,
Each field with local name, not marked on maps,
How come by, how begotten,
Long since forgotten:
Clement's, the Roundabout, Black Mead and Bitter Docks
Rough Shepherd, Horses' Houghs,
And trod the path that grew into this lane
Bending between the hedgerows, where
Convenience claimed a road,—for country road
Is natural growth, with here a curve
Skirting a tree felled long ago, a swerve
To let the rattling harrow pass, the wain
With trussed and swaying load
Lurch safely by, and empty pass again.

He tills the soil to-day,
Surly and grave, his difficult wage to earn.
Cities of discontent, the sickened nerve,
Are still a fashion that he will not learn.
His way is still the obstinate old way,
Even though his horses stare above the hedge,
And whinny, while the tractor drives its wedge
Where they were wont to serve,
And iron robs them of their privilege.
Still is his heart not given
To such encroachments on a natural creed;
Not wholly given, though he bows to need
By urgency and competition driven,
And vanity, to follow with the tide.
Still with a secret triumph he will say,
"Tractor for sand, maybe, but horse for clay,"
And in his calling takes a stubborn pride
That nature still defeats
The frowsty science of the cloistered men,
Their theory, their conceits;
The faith within him still derides the pen,
Experience his text-book. What have they,

The bookish townsmen in their dry retreats,   *Yeoman*
Known to December dawns, before the sun
Reddened the east, and fields were wet and grey?
When have they gone, another day begun,
By tracks into a quagmire trodden,
With sacks about their shoulders and the damp
Soaking until their very souls were sodden,
To help a sick beast, by a flickering lamp,
With rough words and kind hands?
Or felt their boots so heavy and so swere
With trudging over cledgy lands,
Held fast by earth, being to earth so near?

Book-learning they have known.
They meet together, talk, and grow most wise,
But they have lost, in losing solitude,
Something,—an inward grace, the seeing eyes,
The power of being alone;
The power of being alone with earth and skies,
Of going about a task with quietude,
Aware at once of earth's surrounding mood
And of an insect crawling on a stone.

SPRING

THE PEDDLER and the reddleman
   Go vagrant through the shires.
    The peddler tempts the farmer's wife
With all she most admires,
With beads, and boxes made of shells,
With lace and huckaback,
Buckles for shoes and rings for ears,
And Old Moore's Almanack,
With tapes and bobbins, pins and thread,
"What lack you? what d'you lack?"

The reddleman from head to foot
Dyed in his scarlet dye,
Leans like the Devil on the gate,
And grins when children cry.
"Redd for your sheep today, shepherd?
Redd for your yoes and rams?
I never broke a tup's leg yet
Or scared the mothering dams.
You'll find me natty at my job,
And gentle with the lambs."

Fraternity

33

Fraternity

The tinker and the boggart both
Long since have learnt by rote
How cold the rain and sharp the wind
Drive through a ragged coat.
The tinker with his little cart
Hawking his tinny wares,
Puts down his head against the sleet
And whimpers for repairs.
"Kind lady, patch your pots and pans,
And mend your broken chairs?"

The boggart on the frosty ridge,
His sleeveless arms held wide,
Stands gaunt against the wintry sky
Forever crucified,
A raven perched upon his hat,
About his feet the crows.
How bleak December turns the fields,
How desolate the snows,
How long the nights and short the days,
Tatterdemalion knows.

Spring

There's no beginning to the farmer's year,
Only recurrent patterns on a scroll
Unwinding; only use in step with need,
Sharp on the minute when the minute's come;
A watching, waiting thole,
A reckoning by rule-of-thumb.
You may see wealden farmers plough for seed
Before July is out, or dung and drudge
Midsummer yet being here,
Using the drought to carry horse and wain,
Else sinks the hoof to the fetlock, axles strain,
Tines choke. Let farmers do as farmers judge.

Therefore let no man say, "Peas shall be sown
This month or that; now shall the harrow go;
Now scuffle with deep coulters, now with shallow;
Wheat shall succeed to clover; oats to fallow;
Roots after wheat be grown";

Such arbitrary dates and rules are vain;   *Spring*
Not thus the year's arithmetic is planned,
But to outwit the cunning of the land
That will not yield, and will not yield again
Her due of food and wealth
Unless the moment's twisted to its use,
Wrung to the utmost by a vigilant hand,
Admitting no unseasonable excuse.

Nevertheless with spring come certain tasks,   *Sowing*
The sowing of crops, as last year's store sinks low.   *of Crops*
Watch for the day when well-conditioned tilth,
Run by the winter frost, made sweet by rain,—
Crumbles beneath the foot, and warmly basks
In open fields between the budding shaws;
Such time when first the rainbow spans its arch
And settling plover wheel, and ragged daws
Firk on the plough, in the first fair days of March,
With the faint tinkle of a wether's bell;
Days when the sky is wide and pale,
Washed by shed rain, swept clear of cloud
By a forgotten gale;
Bare twiggy copses, uplands newly ploughed,
Cart-tracks, gate-gaps in hedges, everything
Wearing its winter aspect with a difference
Not visible to eye, (not visible
Save in close seeing, in the burgeoning
Of a myriad black and thorny joints,)
Still spare and wintry to the outward eye,
But with what change to the sense,
What readiness, what waiting! the suspense
Of earth laid open, naked to the spring.
Such days as these the wary man appoints
For sowing where his earlier foresight tilled,
And harrows cleared the ground of couch and stones.
Yet will his patience still endure delay
If weather's contrary; let boisterous March go by,
And even April temper into May
Before he entrusts the furrow straitly drilled
With precious grain. He knows the clay,

Sowing
of crops

Malevolent, unkind, a spiteful slave;
Has he not felt its rancour in his bones?
Gashed it with share and mattock? torn its flesh?
Has he not stood beside some new-dug grave
In that same churchyard where himself shall lie
And seen the yellow pit? the clods turned fresh?
And shall he entrust his summer's hope, his pence,
His cattle's fodder, and his children's bread,
Rashly to that inhospitable bed?
No, rather shall he leave his land unsown
A month or more, if acres will not dry.
Occasion's always timely, not so haste;
And month from month takes many an usurer's loan.
So, with his pocket full of tricks,
His dodges girded on, his cunning braced,
He waits his time, to master and defeat,
For he, like other men, must live by politics.
Thus, if the autumn rains have drowned his wheat,
He shall put oats in April in its stead;
Or if a field be obstinate in weeds,
Set clearing crops from February to June:
Roots that will shelter partidges, and swedes,
And mangolds orange as the harvest-moon.
So shall he fill his barns and build his ricks,
Sowing in spring his barley, oats, and seeds,
(But in the autumn, wheat, and the neglected rye,)

Rotation
of crops

And ever shall he bear in mind the art
Known to the Roman, of a changing crop,
To keep his land in kindly heart,
Following wheat on clover, roots on grain,
Fallow on cereal, as he judges best
To mend his weary land and give it rest,
And spare the toiling of his horse and cart
With dung to spread. So shall he make his gain
And please his fields, and profits shall not drop
Nor men be idle.

Hops

               Yet another care,
The pruning and the training of the hop,
Busies the farmer while the year is young.
When bines are cut and cleaned, and poles are bare,

And the loam is richly black with farmyard dung,   *Hops*
Then comes the pruning-knife, and severs clean
Unwanted shoots; the young, too prodigal green
Falls cut, and sadly wilts
There on the ground; but then with balls of twine
Come men on high, strapped stilts,
Woodenly walking, taller than the poles,
Pocking the ground with small round holes,
To tie the string to train the chosen bine,
With a little crawling gang of boys
Busily tying in amongst the hills.
But all's not over then; the rapid plant
Wreathing its spiral upright or aslant,
This delicate tendrilled thing, this English vine
Has baleful foes that prey:
Aphis, that bitter poison kills,
And mould, that sulphur-dust destroys.
So against knave and thief
Work with unsparing hand your sulphur spray,
In early morning when the dew
Lies on the sickened leaf,
Till the clean air with yellow powder fills,
And the bare garden floats in dusty gold;
Not once, but be you watchful to renew
Strife against insect, battle against mould.

Look to your orchards in the early spring   *Orchards*
The blossom-weevil bores into the sheath,
Grubs tunnel in the pith of promising shoots,
The root-louse spends his winter tucked beneath
Rough bark of trunks or chinks of tangled roots;
Canker, rot, scab, and mildew blight the tree;
There seems an enemy in everything.
Even the bullfinch with his pretty song,
And blue puffed tits make havoc in the pears
Pecking with tiny beak and strong;
Mild February airs
Are full of rogues on mischievous wing,
And orchard trees are wickedly tenanted

Orchards

By crawling pirates newly roused from sloth,
The apple-sucker and wood-leopard moth;
Who'd win his fight must wage a constant war,
Have sense in his fingers, eyes behind his head;
Therefore let foresight race ahead of time,
Spray close and well
With soap and sulphur, quassia, lead, and lime,
When buds begin to swell,
All to defeat some small conspirator.

Sometimes in apple country you may see
A ghostly orchard standing all in white,
Aisles of white trees, white branches, in the green,
On some still day when the year hangs between
Winter and spring, and heaven is full of light.
And rising from the ground pale clouds of smoke
Float through the trees and hang upon the air,
Trailing their wisps of blue like a swelled cloak
From the round cheeks of breezes. But though fair
To him who leans upon the gate to stare
And muse "How delicate in spring they be,
That mobled blossom and that wimpled tree,"
There is a purpose in the cloudy aisles
That took no thought of beauty for its care.
For here's the beauty of all country miles,
Their rolling pattern and their space:
That there's a reason for each changing square,
Here sleeping fallow, there a meadow mown,
All to their use ranged different each year,
The shaven grass, the gold, the brindled roan,
Not in some search for empty grace,
But fine through service and intent sincere.

Young
Stock

Nor shall you for your fields neglect your stock;
Spring is the season when the young things thrive,
Having the kindly months before them. Lambs,
Already sturdy, straggle from the flock;
Frisk tails; tug grass-tufts; stare at children; prance;
Then panic-stricken scuttle for their dams.
Calves learn to drink from buckets; foals

Trot laxly in the meadow, with soft glance *Young*
Inquisitive; barn, sty and shed *Stock*
Teem with young innocence newly come alive.
Round collie puppies, on the sunny step,
Buffet each other with their duffer paws
And pounce at flies, and nose the plaited skep,
And with tucked tail slink yelping from the hive.
Likewise the little secret beasts
That open eyes on a world of death and dread,
Thirst, hunger, and mishap,
The covert denizens of holts and shaws,
The little creatures of the ditch and hedge,
Mice nested in a tussock, shrews, and voles,
Inhabitants of the wood,
The red-legged dabchick, paddling in the sedge,
Followed by chubby brood;
The vixen, prick-eared for the first alarm
Beside her tumbling cubs at foot of tree,—
All in the spring begin their precarious round,
Not cherished as the striplings on the farm,
Sheltered, and cosseted, and kept from harm,
But fang and claw against them, snare and trap,
For life is perilous to the small wild things,
Danger's their lot, and fears abound;
Great cats destroy unheedful wings,
And nowhere's safety on the hunted ground;
And who's to blame them, though they be
Sly, as a man would think him shame?
Man in security walks straight and free,
And shall not measure blame,
For they, that each on other preys,
Weasel on rabbit, owl on shrew,
Their cowardly and murderous ways
In poor defence of life pursue,
Not for a wanton killing, not for lust,
As stags will fight among the trampled brake
With antlers running red; with gore and thrust,
With hoofs that stamp, and royal heads that shake
Blood from their eyes,—in vain,
Since still their splendid anger keeps them blind,

Young
Stock

And lowers their entangled brows again,
For brief possession of a faithless hind;—
Not thus, but furtive through the rustling leaves
Life preys on little life; the frightened throat
Squeals once beneath the yellow bite of stoat,
Destroyers all, necessity of kind;
Talon rips fur, and fang meets sharper fang,
And even sleeping limbs must be alert.
But fortunate, if death with sudden pang
Leaps, and is ended; if no lingering hurt,
Dragging a broken wing or mangled paw,
Brings the slow anguish that no night reprieves,
In the dark refuge of a lonely shaw.

So do they venture on their chance of life
When months seem friendliest; so shall men
Repair their herds in spring by natural law
In byre and farrowing pen.
Thus shall you do, with calves that you would rear,
—Heifer, not driven to the slaughterer's knife,
And bull-calf, early cut from bull to steer,—
Two to one udder run, till they may feed
Alone; then turn the little foster-siblings out;
Or wean from birth, and teach to drink from pail,
With fair allowance of their mother's milk,
(But watch, for as the calf grows hale,
He's rough, and knocks the empty pail about.)
By either method shall you safely breed
Moist muzzles, thrifty coats of silk,
Well-uddered heifers, bullocks strong and stout.

Bee-
Master

The wise man, too, will keep his stock of bees
In a sheltered corner of his garden patch,
Where they may winter warmly, breed and hatch
New swarms to fill his combs and fertilize his trees.

I have known honey from the Syrian hills
Stored in cool jars; the wild acacia there
On the rough terrace where the locust shrills,
Tosses her spindrift to the ringing air;

Narcissus bares his nectarous perianth   *Bee-*
In white and golden tabard to the sun,   *Master*
And while the workers rob the amaranth
Or scarlet windflower low among the stone
Intent upon their crops,
The Syrian queens mate in the high hot day,
Rapt visionaries of creative fray,
Soaring from fecund ecstasy alone,
While through the blazing ether, drops
Like a small thunderbolt the vindicated drone.

I have known bees within the ruined arch
Of Akbar's crimson city hang their comb;
Swarm in forsaken courts in a sultry March,
Where the mild ring-doves croon, and small apes play,
And the thin mangy jackal makes his home;
And where, the red walls kindling in the flares,
Once the great Moghul lolling on his throne,
Between his languid fingers crumbling spice,
Ordered his women to the chequered squares,
And moved them at the hazard of the dice.

But this is the bee-master's reckoning
In England. Walk among the hives and hear.

Forget not bees in winter, though they sleep,
For winter's big with summer in her womb,
On the rough terrace where the locust shrills,
And when you plant your rose-trees, plant them deep,
Having regard to bushes all aflame,
And see the dusky promise of their bloom
In small red shoots, and let each redolent name—
Tuscany, Crested Cabbage, Cottage Maid—
Load with full June November's dank repose;
See the kind cattle drowsing in the shade,
And hear the bee about his amorous trade,
Brown in the gipsy crimson of the rose.

In February, if the days be clear,
The waking bee, still drowsy on the wing,
Will guess the opening of another year

41

Bee-
Master

And blunder out to seek another spring.
Crashing through winter sunlight's pallid gold,
His clumsiness sets catkins on the willow
Ashake like lambs' tails in the early fold,
Dusting with pollen all his brown and yellow,
But when the rimy afternoon turns cold
And undern squalls buffet the chilly fellow,
He'll seek the hive's warm waxen welcoming
And set about the chambers' classic mould.

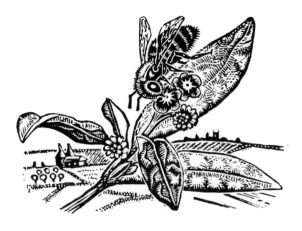

And then pell-mell his harvest follows swift,
Blossom and borage, lime and balm and clover,
On Downs the thyme, on cliffs the scantling thrift,
Everywhere bees go racing with the hours,
For every bee becomes a drunken lover,
Standing upon his head to sup the flowers.
All over England, from Northumbrian coasts,
To the wild sea-pink blown on Devon rocks,
Over the merry southern gardens, over
The grey-green bean-fields, round the Kentish oasts,
Through the frilled spires of cottage hollyhocks,
Go the big brown fat bees, and wander in
Where dusty spears of sunlight cleave the barn,
And seek the sun again, and storm the whin,
And in the warm meridian solitude
Hum in the heather round the moorland tarn.

Look, too, when summer hatches out the brood,

In tardy May or early June,   *Bee-*
And the young queens are strong in the cocoon,   *Master*
Watch, if the days be warm,
The flitting of the swarm.
Follow, for if beyond your sight they stray,
Your bees are lost, and you must take your way
Homeward disconsolate; but be at hand
And you may take your bees on strangers' land.
Have your skep ready, drowse them with your smoke;
Whether they cluster on the handy bough
Or in the difficult hedge, be nimble now,
For bees are captious folk
And quick to turn against the lubber's touch,
But if you shake them to their wicker hutch
Firmly, and turn towards the hive your skep,
Into the hive the clustered thousands stream,
Mounting the little slatted sloping step,
A ready colony, queen, workers, drones,
Patient to build again the waxen thrones
For younger queens, and all the chambered cells
For lesser brood, and all the immemorial scheme.

And still they labour, though the hand of man
Inscrutable and ravaging descend,
Pillaging in their citadels,
Defeating wantonly their provident plan,
Making a havoc of their patient hoard;
Still silly bees, not knowing to what end,
Not knowing to what ultimate reward
Or what new ruin of the garnered hive
The senseless god in man will send,
Still in blind stupid industry will strive,
Constructing for destruction pitiably,
That still their unintelligible lord
May reap his wealth from their calamity.

White virgin honey comes from earliest flowers,
White virgin honey in the market prized;
From the white clover creeping in the field,
From orchard-blossom that the worker scours,

43

Bee- *Master*	—The richest honey-flow of all the Weald,— But cottage-gardens shall not be despised Here where no heather is, and scanty lime; Therefore, at evening, when the field-work's done, And daylight lingers with the latening sun, Let gardeners too remember sowing-time.
Gardener	When skies are gentle, breezes bland, When loam that's warm within the hand Falls friable between the tines, Sow hollyhocks and columbines, The tufted pansy, and the tall Snapdragon in the broken wall, Not for this summer, but for next, Since foresight is the gardener's text, And though his eyes may never know How lavishly his flowers blow, Others will stand and musing say "These were the flowers he sowed that May."

But for this summer's quick delight
Sow marigold, and sow the bright
Frail poppy that with noonday dies
But wakens to a fresh surprise;
Along the pathway stones be set
Sweet Alysson and mignonette,
That when the full midsummer's come
On scented clumps the bees may hum,
Golden Italians, and the wild
Black humble-bee alike beguiled:
And lovers who have never kissed
May sow the cloudy Love-in-Mist.

Nor be the little space forgot
For herbs to spice the kitchen pot:
Mint, pennyroyal, bergamot,
Tarragon and melilot,
Dill for witchcraft, prisoner's rue,
Coriander, costmary,
Tansy, thyme, Sweet Cicely,

Saffron, balm, and rosemary   *Gardener*
That since the Virgin threw her cloak
Across it,—so say cottage folk—
Has changed its flowers from white to blue.
But have a care that seeds be strewn
One night beneath a waxing moon,
And pick when the moon is on the wane,
Else shall your toil be all in vain.

She walks among the loveliness she made,   *The*
Between the apple-blossom and the water—   *Island*
She walks among the patterned pied brocade,
Each flower her son, and every tree her daughter.
This is an island all with flowers inlaid,
A square of grassy pavement tessellated;
Flowers in their order blowing as she bade,
And in their company by her created.
The waving grasses freckle sun with shade,
The wind-blown waters round the kingcups ripple,
Colour on colour chequered and arrayed,
Shadow on light in variable stipple.
Her regiments at her command parade,
Foot-soldier primrose in his rank comes trooping,
Then wind-flowers in a scarlet loose brigade,
Fritillary with dusky orchis grouping.
They are the Cossacks, dim in ambuscade,
Scarfed in their purple like a foreign stranger,
Piratical, and apt for stealthy raid,
Wherever's mystery or doubtful danger.
Iris salutes her with his broad green blade,
And marches by with proud imperial pennant,
And tulips in a flying cavalcade
Follow valerian for their lieutenant.
The Lords-and-Ladies dressed for masquerade
In green silk domino discreetly hooded,
Hurry towards the nut-trees' colonnade,
Philandering where privacy's well wooded;
They're the civilians of this bold crusade,
The courtiers of this camp by blossom tented,
With woodbine clambering the balustrade,

The
Island

And all by briar roses battlemented.
There, in the sunlit grasses green as jade,
She walks; she sees her squadrons at attention,
And, laughing at her flowery escapade,
Stretches her hands towards her dear invention.

The wild
flowers

This much of gardens; but I tell
Also of native flowers in wood and dell;
Not such as, sudden on a stony height,
Break from the warmth of snow and live in light
Of mountain sun on Alp or Dolomite,
Bright squabs on limestone screes;
Not of the Rhoetian poppy, fluttering brave
Frail yellow flags beside a rocky track
Alone with eagles; not of these,
Not of the thymes that greenly pave
A fallen cliff, rock-rose in cruel crack;
Not of the scarlet tulip, slim and bright,
Snapped by the gallop of the wild gazelle;
But of such flowers as dwell
In marsh and meadow, wayside, wood and waste,
Of campion and the little pimpernel;
Of kexen parsley and the varied vetch;
Of the living mesh, cats-cradle in a ditch;
Of gorse and broom and whins;
Of hops and buckwheat and the wild woodbine
That with their stems must twine
Like the way of the sun to left from right;
Of berried bindweeds, twisting widdershins;
Of all the tangle of the hedgerow, laced
With thorny dog-rose and the deadly dwale;
Throughout the seasons do I count their tale,
But orderly, that those who walk abroad

The wood-
flowers

In lane and wood
May find them in their season as they grow;
Anemones like some last drift of snow
Between the hazels, hanging down their bell
When rain's about; small woodruff low;
Bugles, that leave the shelter of the glade
And march across the open; violets that blow

Purple and dim at tree's-foot; and the tall   *The wood-*
Orchis that country children call   *flowers*
By many names, some pretty and some rude.
These are the flowers that shelter in the wood
Sulky in colour, secret in the shade;
But wayside tramps, saucy and unafraid,   *The*
Jack-by-the hedge, Pickpocket, Ragged Robin,   *wayside*
Small yellows and small scarlets, nowise strange,   *flowers*
Nowise like aliens strayed,
But English and robust,
Fight tangled for their life, through grit and dust,
Pushing their way with spring, when heifers range
Uneasy up the lane, and as they go
Tug at a passing mouthful, biting harsh.
And others in the meadow and the marsh
Make rings round Easter; kingcup, marigold,
And the pale orchis dappled like a dobbin;
Buttercups thousand-fold
Wearing their cloth-of-gold among the hay
With clover and the little eye-of-day.

Once I went through the lanes, over the sharp   *Fritil-*
Tilt of the little bridges; past the forge,   *laries*
And heard the clang of anvil and of iron,
And saw the founting sparks in the dusky forge,
And men outside with horses, gossiping.
So I came through that April England, moist
And green in its lush fields between the willows,
Foaming with cherry in the woods and pale
With clouds of lady's-smock along the hedge,
Until I came to a gate and left the road
For the gentle fields that enticed me, by the farms,
Wandering through the embroidered fields, each one
So like its fellow; wandered through the gaps,
Past the mild cattle knee-deep in the brooks,
And wandered drowsing as the meadows drowsed
Under the pale wide heaven and slow clouds.
And then I came to a field where the springing grass
Was dulled by the hanging cups of fritillaries,
Sullen and foreign-looking, the snaky flower,

Fritil-
laries

Scarfed in dull purple, like Egyptian girls
Camping among the furze, staining the waste
With foreign colour, sulky, dark, and quaint,
Dangerous too, as a girl might sidle up,
An Egyptian girl, with an ancient snaring spell,
Throwing a net, soft round the limbs and heart,
Captivity soft and abhorrent, a close-meshed net,
—See the square web on the murrey flesh of the flower—
Holding her captive close with her bare brown arms,
Close to her little breast beneath the silk,
A gipsy Judith, witch of a ragged tent,
And I shrank from the English field of fritillaries
Before it should be too late, before I forgot
The cherry white in the woods, and the curdled clouds,
And the lapwings crying free above the plough.

Spring

The spring was late that year, I well remember,
The year when first I came on the field of fritillaries;
So late, the cottars meeting in the lanes
Would stop to marvel mildly, with that old
Unplumbed capacity for wonderment
At Nature's whim. The calendar told spring,
But spring was heedless: April into May
Passed, and the trees still wore their livery
Of lean black winter's servants; very strange
Most lovely Easter played three days at summer,
A heavy summer over winter's fields,
Three days, and then was vanished, like a queen
Dropping the lifted flap of her pavilion.

Nightly I leant me at the window-sill,
Telling the chaplet of the slipping days,
But still the lamp streamed wet on polished stones,
And still the nights were empty silences
Robbed of the nightingale; they only held
The slanting strings of rain: Orion marched
Invisible down the hours from dusk to dawn,
Till morning pallor lost him, but the clouds
Hid all his gradual latening; that year
He shot his midnight javelins unseen

And dipped the horizon into other skies,   *Spring*
Lost to the North, till autumn should renew
His captaincy, with Rigel, Betelgeuse,
Aldebaran, and brightest Sirius.

Have we so many springs allotted us,
And who would rob a pauper of his pence?

Then broke the spring. The hedges in a day
Burgeoned to green; the drawing of the trees,
Incomparably pencilled line by line,
Thickened to heaviness, and men forgot
The intellectual austerity
Of winter, in the rich warm-blooded rush
Of growth, and mating beasts, and rising sap.
How swift and sudden strode that tardy spring,
Between a sunrise and a sunset come!
The shadow of a swallow crossed the wall;
Nightingales sang by day. The pushing blade
Parted the soil. The morning roofs and oasts
There, down the lane, beside the brook and willows,
Cast their long shadows. Pasture, ankle-wet,
Steamed to the sun. The tulips dyed their green
To red in cottage gardens. Bees astir,
Fussing from flower to flower, made war on time.
Body and blood were princes; the cold mind
Sank with Orion from the midnight sky;
The stars of spring rose visible: The Virgin;
Al Fard the solitary; Regulus
The kingly star, the handle of the Sickle;
And Venus, lonely splendour in the west,
Roamed over the rapt meadows; shone in gold
Beneath the cottage eaves where nesting birds
Obeyed love's law; shone through the cottage panes
Where youth lay sleeping on the breast of youth,
Where love was life, and not a brief desire;
Shone on the heifer blaring for the bull
Over the hedgerow deep in dewy grass:
And glinted through the dark and open door
Where the proud stallion neighing to his mares

Spring Stamped on the cobbles of the stable floor.
For all were equal in the sight of spring,
Man and his cattle; corn; and greening trees,
Ignorant of the soul's perplexity,
Ignorant of the wherefore and the end,
Bewildered by no transient ecstasy,
But following the old and natural law,
Nor marred nor blazing with a royal excess;
The law of life and life's continuance.

That was a spring of storms. They prowled the night;
Low level lightning flickered in the east
Continuous. The white pear-blossom gleamed
Motionless in the flashes; birds were still;
Darkness and silence knotted to suspense,
Riven by the premonitory glint
Of skulking storm, a giant that whirled a sword
Over the low horizon, and with tread
Earth-shaking ever threatened his approach,
But to delay his terror kept afar,
And held earth stayed in waiting like a beast
Bowed to receive a blow. But when he strode
Down from his throne of hills upon the plain,
And broke his anger to a thousand shards

Over the prostrate fields, then leapt the earth   *Spring*
Proud to accept his challenge; drank his rain;
Under his sudden wind tossed wild her trees;
Opened her secret bosom to his shafts;
The great drops spattered; then above the house
Crashed thunder, and the little wainscot shook
And the green garden in the lightning lay.

Who has not seen the spring, is blind, is dead.
Better for him that he should coffined lie,
And in that coin his toll to Nature pay
Than live a debtor. All things shall pass by
That fret his mind: the shift of policy,
Princes' ambition, wiser governance,
Civilisation's tides. There's dissonance
By our great necessary Babel bred,
Perplexes eager spirits unprepared,
Puts out their seeing eyes, leaves their blind touch
To grope past prejudice and ignorance
Towards solution, as they throw away
Each broken, each successive crutch.
Such truths as we have snared
Into the spread conspiracy of our nets,
Come to us fragmentary from a whole,
As meteorites from space. Now science sets
Two splintered ends together, makes one shred
Corroborate another; now live flesh
Persuades us by its drunken fallacy;
Now the instinctive soul
Takes its short-cut to grace; now blown by gust
Of hazard, truth's entangled in strange mesh,
Else how should poetry,
The runes of divination, superstition
Fastening sharp claw on common circumstance,
Even artifice as neat astrology
Twisting the very stars to fit man's ends,
Mingle some ore with dross of sorcery
Unless the fragment of the whole be part?
There's some relation we may not adjust,
Some concord of creation that the mind

Spring   Only in perilous balance apprehends,
Loth, fugitive, obscure.
All else dies in its season; all perplexities,
Even human grief with human body dies,
Such griefs that press so wildly on the heart
As to crush in its shell. But still endure
Nature's renewal and man's fortitude,
A common thing, a permanent common thing,
So coarse, so stated, usual, and so rude,
So quiet in performance, and so slow
That hurrying wit outruns it. Yet with spring
Life leaps; her fountains flow;
And nimble foolish wit must humbled go.

There were so many days that I was given.
But whether of this spring or that? they merge
As travelling clouds across my permanent heaven.

My life was rich; I took a swarm of bees
And found a crumpled snake-skin on the road,
All in one day, and was increased by these.

I have not understood humanity.
But those plain things, that gospel of each year,
Made me the scholar of simplicity.

> *This once I saw, but not again,*
> *Above the water pocked by rain:*
> *Three mottled eggs in a moorhen's nest,*
> *In a clump of kingcups by the edge*
> *Of the water, in amongst the sedge;*
> *The rain was but an April shower;*
> *The kingcup but a minted flower,*
> *Cup of a king in gold.*
> *Was there not once a king who sought him*
> *The perfect chalice, and bethought him*
> *The breast of Helen for his mould?*
> *A wild bird's nest and Helen's breast,*
> *What lovely things that spring did hold!*

★

Now die the sounds. No whisper stirs the trees.   *Nocturne*
  Her pattern merged into the general web
The shriven day accepts her obsequies
  With humble ebb.

Now are the noiseless stars made visible
  That hidden by the day pursued their track,
And this one planet that we know too well
  Mantles in black.

Then, from the thicket, sang the nightingale,
  So wildly sweet, so sudden, and so true,
It seemed a herald from beyond the veil
  Had broken through.

The common earth's confusion all unseen,
  But worlds revealed in broad magnificence,—
That unembodied music thrid between
  Sprang hence, or thence?

Nothing remained of the familiar round,
  Only the soul ecstatic and released
Founted towards the spheres in jets of sound,
  And died, and ceased,

But plangent from the thickets of the thorn
  Broke other voices, taking up the choir,
While Cancer interlaced with Capricorn
  In silent fire,

And all the harmonies were joined and whole,
  Silence was music, music silence made,
Till each was both or either, and the soul
  Was not afraid.

SUMMER

NOW BE YOU THANKFUL, who in England dwell,
    That to the starving trees and thirsty grass
    Even at summer's height come cloudy fleets
Moist from the wastes of the Atlantic swell,
To spill their rain, and pass,
While fields renew their sweets.
Not as the Arab watches in despair
The scrannel promise of his harvest parch
Even before the sun climbs high in March
And only dust-motes dim the scorching air.
He who must yoke to wooden water-wheel
The bullock or the camel, turning slow
But constant in the round and trodden groove,
Slumberous as hypnotics move,
To the lamentation of the whining cogs,
While in the runnels rapid waters flow,
Lapped by the timid tongue of pariah dogs,
And in the trenches spread, to quench and heal.
Or as the Persian from his hills of snow,
Gathers the freshet to the jealous pool,

And floods his garden with a hundred streams
Under the plane-trees when the evening's cool,
But still for all his pains
Sees roses languish with returning noon,
And in the heat of June
The leaves already flutter from the planes.

Such arid months as only exiles know,
With longing for the smell of English rains,
Some drops to lay the dust, some shower to stir
The earthy redolence of soaking loam,
Some saddening of the sky before the shower,
Some dew to hold a footprint for an hour;
When through the stones the lizard and the snake
Rustle their brittle length, and crickets chirr
Day after day, and broom-pods crackling break,
Scavenger kites hang waiting for the dead
Over the old and solitary ram,
And the mule picks his way up the dried river-bed,—
This know, and know then how the heart can ache
With pining for the woods and clouds of home.

If I could take my England, and could wring
One living moment from her simple year,
One moment only, whether of place or time,
—One winter coppice feathery with rime,
One shred of dawn in spring,—
Then should my voice find echo in English ear;
Then might I say, "That which I love, I am."

Full summer comes; June brings the longest day
All country dwellers know the small despair
Of the year's summit; but the yeoman now
Has little time for vain regrets to spare.
There's work enough for him and all his folks;
He watches for the flowering of his hay;
Knows that cleared land is ready for the plough;
Washes his empty sheds with cleansing lime
While herds at pasture fatten to their prime,
With fisking tails in shade beneath the oaks.

And before great harvest takes him to the field, *Sheep*
Imperious and urgent for his time, *Shearing*
If he be wise he'll finish with his flock
Shearing as early as the warmth of May
Down in the genial meadows of the Weald.
There, in a barn, with crazy doors swung wide
Making a square of sun on dusty floor,
The shearer sits, in shepherd's borrowed smock,
And from the pen of huddled backs outside,
Each beast in turn is driven through the door;
Struggles, and kicks, but with a hands-twist thrown
Lies foolish, as the fingers slick and deft
Open the fleece and cut the belly up,
(Changing left hand for right, and right for left,)
Against the fall of wool, in one sole piece,
All test of skill, all source of surly pride;
Then on the heap is pitched the greasy fleece,
And the clipped sheep,—hogg, wether, lusty tup,—
Staggers astonished from such curt release,
And bleating seeks the refuge of the heft;
Naked, and bleating, and at first forlorn
With narrow smear of blood on neck or side,
From sharp experience goes the shearling shorn.

Yet is the shepherd roughly kind; *Shepherd*
Anoints a wound, shakes disapproving head,
But tolerant, to slight mishap resigned;
Scours the short wool for maggot, tick, or ked.
Shepherd's an old and a familiar trade;
Abel, that firstling of the sunburnt plains,
Through the scorched months between the annual rains
Sang to his firstlings in the fig-tree's shade;
As Jacob, seven years to win a maid,
—She being beautiful, and Leah but tender-eyed,—
Drove out his flock into the stony place,
Ringstraked, speckled, pied;
Peeled the green poplar switch, and dreamed of
    Rachel's face;
A David, young and ruddy, kept the sheep,
Shepherd and harp-player in the wilderness;

Shepherd   Shaping for kingship, growing to a throne,
Come from the wilds to soothe dark Saul to sleep.
For no man knows as he who lives alone
The vigour of a purpose deeply laid,
The strength, the fate, the seal upon his brow,
The urgency of an unpublished vow,
A vow unregistered, a vow unmade,
Unknown to its maker, rather; only known
To the God and origin of such fumbling ends,
So inly lived, so congruously held,
True in each gesture as by force compelled,
(For no man sees the pattern of his maze,
Least of all he who plans his careful ways
Lacking the strong inevitable thing,)
As Israel, Abel, David knew,
Yet unaware to consummation grew,
The patriarch, the martyr, and the king.

No man is closer to the beasts he tends,
Nor, idle, savours such contented days;
No man more blessèd-free,
From our need of comfort and of friends,
Love, props, illusion, counterfeit, escape;
Living a life that to its real shape
Evolves, increases, swells its girth, ascends,
As an unconscious and a splendid tree,
A fact of Nature, not a random plan.

I remember, I met two shepherds carrying
An old man, dead, high on the summer Downs.
He was a shepherd too; I had known the man.
Foxes he knew, he knew the ways of the hawk,
The ways of the weather, but not the ways of towns.
Dead now, his white flock going before
With shaken bells across the scars of chalk,
His dog at heel of the man who propped his head.
I stopped to gaze, since I should gaze no more;
To take my last look, since here was no returning,
But could not learn from him, for there's no learning
Either from alien or familiar dead.

After the general shearing still remain
The tenderer milch-yoes to be clipped.
A separate job, some later week,
When temperate days will hold,
—For eild sheep, wethers, hoggs, and barren yoes
Risk with less danger the returning cold.
Then may the lambs be dipped,
The lambs that frantic for their mothers seek
Who gaunt, ungainly, queer, regain the fold.
And general dipping next in order goes,
Snatched between hay and harvest, as may be,
And as the ripening and the weather fit.
This is a feast that makes the whole farm shout
With laughter as on holiday, to see
The bothered and unwilling beasts submit
And swim the tank, and scramble dripping out
With never a maggot left, or louse, or flea.
Sheep do the work, while men stand grinning by,
Knowing that work in earnest waits them after
This interlude, this funning, and this laughter,
Work in the fields, with aching thews, and sweat,
And blessed coolth only when sun has set.

Sheep
Washing

The summer's horn indeed is full with crops;
And earlier toil its due reward has earned.
Now shall you reap and gather, store and stack
Your hay, your corn, your barley and your hops
In close succession, being less concerned
With calendar and farmer's almanac
Than with good timely weather, setting fair
Over the parcelled fields from copse to copse;
Good summer sun, that dries the waggon track,
Ripens the grasses, tans the swollen awn
And puts contented faces everywhere.

Haysel
and
Harvest

First you shall cut your hay, when grasses stand
In flower, but running not to seed,
But even here rehearse the farmer's creed:
'Tis farmer, not the date, that calls the tune;
Better dry August hay than wet in June.

Haysel

59

Haysel

Have your folks working in the fields by dawn,
Your team of horses doubly spanned;
Leave the cut swath all day; and air by rake
Next morning, and, if weather still be set,
Gather to cocks for carting, but should wet
Flatten the cocks, then you shall tedd and shake
Again when sun returns. Now you shall build
Your rick in yard or field, as suits you best,
Choosing your stacker for a good man skilled,
Building on brushwood, sides both true and straight,
That when hay settles lines may still be plumb;
And let each forkful to its place be pressed
And truly bound, by stacker's treading weight;
Widen your eaving-course; let roof be steep,
Bents sloping outwards, so to keep
Rain from the heart until the thatcher come.
Then you may leave your rick with easy mind;
Fodder for sweet-breathed cattle shall be sweet;
And whether nights be harsh or days be kind
Your hay shall neither moulder, rot, nor heat;
You shall not wake to hear your cowman shout,
As calving heifer calls him from his rest;
You shall not stare to see in fear and doubt
A blood-red feather flaming on the west,
And rousing all your people as you run,
Hasten too late towards your labour's pyre,
And see your reckoned trusses, hardly-won,
Blaze to the wanton merriment of fire.

Harvest

Next shall you reap your corn. Your oats shall fall
Before full ripeness set them on to shed,
But leave your barley till it droop the head
With ripened beard. The tall
Wheat for an early cut; at midday, walk
When sun is hot and high, and if you hear
Straw crackle in the standing crop,
And see the slender forest of the stalk
Still green towards the ground, but gold at top,
Then you may know that cutting-time is near.
Peas are pernickety; cut when you may.

Beans, the sweet-scented beans of spring, shall stand
Till pods are turning black, or till you clear
Against the needs of autumn for your land.
Now as to cutting: you shall choose your day
When weather signs are fairest, as for hay;
Scythe first the heading round the field by hand,
Then send your reaper up the flat gold wall
With whirling sails and clash of toppling sheaves:
See that the cutter keen and sharply cleaves,
And that the horses, driven with a level gait,
Work the full width, and keep the measure straight.

And in the evening when the final square
Of standing corn fast dwindles to its end,
When the tired horses take a sharper bend,
A shorter strip each time, as day grows late,
Let boys stand round, with ready stick and stone,
To watch for the dash of rabbit or of hare
Within the last small narrowing refuge penned;
Poor frightened Wat, that all the day alone
(Since first the reaper with its whirring noise
Made terror of the field,)
Crouched to the ground, by friendly straw concealed,

Harvest   Inward and inward creeping, as the voice
Of men came nearer, and the sheaves were thrown
Out on the widening stubble, there to lie
Until the stooker with his fork came by,
And horses' shaggy fetlocks trampled past
At their monotonous pacing, till at last
Through thinning stalks, pressed flat against the earth,
The fugitive saw, with starting eye,
Their shining shoes strike fire on errant flints,
And the sharp knives slip by with level glints.
Then goes the lean brown body for its life,
Streaked for the distant shelter of the wood,
Across the new, strange stubble hurled,
That was not there at dawn,—a different world
Since men and horses came with cutting knife,
And razed the corn that tall and rustling stood.
But odds too heavy end the frantic race;
There's nothing but a twitching body cast
Down by a jacket, as 'twere nothing worth
But shillings to the farmer's frugal wife.

An English cornfield in full harvesting
Is English as the Bible, though no more
(These clanking times) the gleaners following
The reapers by their rhythm rapt
Plunder the gavels for their little store;
Or the sickle cut the poppies and the corn,
Save when the crop is tangled by a gale,
Beaten by rain, twisted like murdered hair:
Then comes the sickle to its old avail
Crook'd as the young moon in her narrowest horn,
And steals in the poor broken tangle, where
Straightforward knives are parried, and the apt
Inventiveness of man shall not prevail.
Then to the simplest shapes of his first craft,
—Livelihood wrested from the earth that bore,
Cradled, and coffined him,—man shall repair;
Shapes copied from the sky, with cutting edge;
Natural shapes, to meet the natural hitch
Of hindering weather, the permanent enemy;

Then, with the noonscape, underneath the hedge,   *Harvest*
His fingers blistered by the rubbing haft,
His shoulders propped by hedge, his feet in ditch,
The random reaper drains his pint of ale.

Look to your stooking, for full many a field
Of hearty grain and straw runs half to waste
Through heedless stooking, and the proper yield
Leaves half its measure to the rook and daw.
But if you'd have full grain and ripened straw,
After a week of drying fit to cart,
Stooker, take up a sheaf in either hand,
Between the ears and band,
And swing them clear, and bring the butts apart
Sharply to ground, ears sloping to a peak,
(Ten sheaves for Kent,) clashing together braced,
So that the little ridge be thatched and sleek,
Firm to the wind, secure to rain and hail,
That winnower and that flail,
Those thieves of harvest, pilfering what they can
In last-hour larceny from rival man.
For nature gives, and nature takes again;
Therefore be eager of her liberal hours;
To drought succeeds the flood, to calm the gale,
And winter's frost lays low the summer's flowers.
Therefore, you harvesters, before the rain
Trample your crop with roguish feet,
Wring what you may, and if too fast and fleet
Even the summer sun describe his arc
Leaving you with your shocks but half-way set,
Be prouder than the punctual rigid clerk,
And stickle not to labour after dark,
For you take nature's orders, he the clock's.
The cooler night shall spare your noonday sweat;
The breeze shall whisper in the rustling shocks;
The moon above the thorn
Rise harvest-tawny on the stubble shorn,
And in the bending lines of girls and men
Some snatch of song be born.
Lovers shall find their magic then,

Harvest   And jolly farmers wink at privilege;
Only the moon shall look behind the hedge,
Confederate of youth;
Only the moon shall hear the whispered pledge,
Great lyric liar, to a lovelier truth
Transcending, setting purport free,
And touching all things with her alchemy.

> *When moonlight reigns, the meanest brick and stone*
> *Take on a beauty not their own,*
> *And past the flaw of builded wood*
> *Shines the intention whole and good,*
> *And all the little homes of man*
> *Rise to a dimmer, nobler plan*
> *When colour's absence gives escape*
> *To the deeper spirit of the shape,*
>
> *— Then earth's great architecture swells*
> *Among her mountains and her fells*
> *Under the moon to amplitude*
> *Massive and primitive and rude,*
>
> *— Then do the clouds like silver flags*
> *Stream out above the tattered crags,*
> *And black and silver all the coast*
> *Marshals its hunched and rocky host,*
> *And headlands striding sombrely*
> *Buttress the land against the sea,*
> *The darkening land, the brightening wave,—*
> *When moonlight slants through Merlin's cave.*

And August comes, when fields are sere and brown,
When stubble takes the place of ruffling corn;
When the sweet grass is like a prisoner shorn;
The air is full of drifting thistledown,
Grey pointed sprites, that on the breezes ride.
The cloyed trees droop, the ash-keys spinning fall;
The brooks are pebbly; for the trickle's dried;
Birds moult, and in the leafy copses hide,
And summer makes a silence after spring,
As who with age a liberal youth should chide.

This is the month of weeds.
Kex, charlock, thistle,
Among the shorn bristle
Of stubble drop seeds.
This is the month of weeds.

Weod-
monath

Spurry, pimpernel, quitch,
Twine in the stubble,
Making for trouble;
With nettle in ditch,
Spurry, pimpernel, quitch.

Yet the field has a friend
The nimble clover,
Custodian, lover,
Yare to defend.
The field has a friend.

Humble-bees boldly reach
Red clover's honey,
Paid in sweet money.
Hive-bees in vain beseech:
Honey is out of reach.

Now let the clover spread;
Nature it craveth;
Foemen it braveth,
Strangling them dead.
So let the clover spread.

Now pasture's low; the moidered cattle-men
Drive their poor stock by unaccustomed paths
To forage on the richer aftermaths,
Old hay-fields, billowy with dip and stetch.
Now by the hedgerows and along the lane
The berried cuckoo-pint and yellow vetch
Herald the autumn, and the squirrels rob
Windfalls of hazel and the Kentish cob,
(Plumping their kernels white as children's teeth,)
With acorns, provender for the winter drey,
That little larder, safely tucked beneath
Leaves, roots, old tree-stumps, for a milder day

Summer

65

Summer   Of winter, when the sleeping muscles stretch
And there's a stirring in the sodden wood
As woken squirrel reaches after food.

Man's not the only harvester; urchins and voles
Lay up their store of berries and of grain
Preciously gleaned and carried to their holes
With busy trotting paws and serious snout,
Each to his schemes no less than man devout,
Making of instinct all-sufficient reasons;
Intent on waking with the spring again
To life's new provocation, as if seasons
Eternally renewed were dedicate
To hedge-hogs, squirrels, badgers, men, mice, moles.

But though such hints of autumn gild the late
Summer, still is the summer fully here,
Great-breasted, brazen, strumpet of the year;
Furiously I do the summer hate,
Resentfully I do the summer love,
The woods all amorous with croodling dove,
Days weakening to the soul, days threatening
Winter-bought strength, thin purity of spring.
With summer's laxness am I all undone.
What can I do in summer? What but sing:

> *Far from shrewd companies,*
> *Far from the flares,*
> *Here where the summer is,*
> *And laden airs,*
> *Here where no noise of men*
> *Down in the wood*
> *Startles the water-hen*
> *And small black brood,*
> *Here where the branches wave*
> *And day is green,*
> *Making the wood a cave*
> *Aquamarine,*
> *Here where the insects hum,*
> *And dragon-fly,*

SUMMER

Here we clandestine come,   *Summer*
Marvell and I.

In summer when the woods are deep,
Ghostly society I keep,
And play the spy, down dappled glades,
On lovely or on ardent shades,
Eavesdropper on the gallant game
Where nothing's burnt by so much flame,
And nothing broken but the rhyme
From maying-time to haying-time.
And what's the matter, though I see
A wrongly amorous company?
Though lover after lover flit
Labelled with names that do not fit?
If Lovelace Sacharissa woo,
Or Waller Julia pursue,
If Marvell do Lucasta find
Than his Own mistress less unkind,
Or Herrick's persuasions prove
A better argument of love
Than the conversion of the Jew?

The cuckoo stutters in his note,
But still the turbulent petticoat
Of cherry silk or oyster grey
Makes lively sport through summer day.
The rounded arm, the bunchèd curl,
The peeping shoe, the sullen pearl,—
Between the trees they glance and pass,
Or take their ease upon the grass.

Perilla, fly! Corinna, stay!
In deserts of Bohemia,
A wood near Athens, or this wood
Where these grown oaks as saplings stood
Three hundred English years gone by,
"And yet I love her till I die."

So, for the idle, float the lither days,
The seremonth deepens as its age draws on;

67

Summer   Morning and evening veil them in a haze;
But when the last high loaded cart has gone
Leaving its trail of straws along the hedge,
And the last mug is drained to harvest-pledge,
Work still remains to finish what is done.

Thatcher   Thatcher with carpet bound about his knees
Tramps farm to farm with slow deliberate stride.
Thatchers are rare, these days, he'd have you know,
Good thatchers, those that go
About their business as it were a pride,
Scorning Dutch barns and mushrooms such as these,
New-fangled, driving out a settled trade.
Once there were thatchers, ah, could hip a roof
Easy as twist a sheaf; were not afraid
Of any rain, since work was weather-proof.
East Anglia bred them, where the reeds grow grey
Mile upon fenny mile, and ducks go home
Over the level wastes of dyke and sluice.
Still maundering on, he sorts his pegs, his comb,
His wooden bat, his twine, in neat array,
Trimming his straw,—full length of wheaten straw,—
Watered and sweated ready to its use,
Sweet in the yelm, for thatch without a flaw.
Grumbling and boasting turn and turn about,
Having told the tally of the needed threaves,
He mounts his ladder, pocket full of splines,
And packs his yelms, and calls his mate a lout
If he disturb one straw from ordered lines.
Proud of his stelch, and prouder of his eaves,
Proud of his skill to thatch an awkward pent,
He is an artist with a long descent,
Brother to workers in peculiar crafts;
To the old wheel-wright, punctual timber-master,
—Could tell you whether wood were frow or doted
Before the trunk was opened; often quoted
The Bible; could turn out a pair of shafts
With straight and proper grain; adzed every spoke
By hand, and never had one cracked or bent;—
Brother to pargetter, with hair and plaster,

68

Combing the diaper on porous lime,   *Craftsmen*
Pleased as a child with patterns he'd invent;
Brother to all the slow fastidious folk
Whose care is matched by their disdain of time;
To basket-makers, shaping Kentish bodges;
To osier-weavers, twisting supple wands;
To Jack-of-all-trades with his sundry dodges;
Brick-layer, even, carrying his hod;
To Down-bred shepherds, puddling secret ponds,
So jealous of their mystery, for dew;
Lastly, to dowser, forcing virgin wells,
That changeling of the willows, simple, odd,
Touched by some finger laid on him askew
At birth by nixie or by water-god;
But dowser never knows, or never tells.
Smiling, the willow upright in his hold,
Vacant he lags across the thirsty miles;
Shall water pull him? or shall buried gold,
Panoply of a Dane, beneath a mound?
But dowser never knew, or never told.
Only, he pauses when he feels the switch
Quicken between his fingers, curtsey, twitch;
Pauses, and points, and smiles,
And loses interest; for water's found.

All craftsmen share a knowledge. They have held
Reality down fluttering to a bench;
Cut wood to their own purposes; compelled
The growth of pattern with the patient shuttle;
Drained acres to a trench.
Control is theirs. They have ignored the subtle
Release of spirit from the jail of shape.
They have been concerned with prison, not escape;
Pinioned the fact, and let the soul go free,
And out of need made inadvertent art.
All things designed to play a faithful part
Build up their plain particular poetry.
Tools have their own integrity;
The sneath of scythe curves rightly to the hand,
The hammer knows its balance, knife its edge,

69

Craftsmen   All tools inevitably planned,
Stout friends, with pledge
Of service; with their crotchets too
That masters understand,
And proper character, and separate heart,
But always to their chosen temper true.
—So language, smithied at the common fire,
Grew to its use; as sneath and shank and haft
Of well-grained wood, nice instruments of craft,
Curve to the simple mould the hands require,
Born of the needs of man.
The poet like the artisan
Works lonely with his tools; picks up each one,
Blunt mallet knowing, and the quick thin blade,
And plane that travels when the hewing's done;
Rejects, and chooses; scores a fresh faint line;
Sharpens, intent upon his chiselling;
Bends lower to examine his design,
If it be truly made,
And brings perfection to so slight a thing.
But in the shadows of his working-place,
Dust-moted, dim,
Among the chips and lumber of his trade,
Lifts never his bowed head, a breathing-space
To look upon the world beyond the sill,
The world framed small, in distance, for to him
The world and all its weight are in his will.
Yet in the ecstasy of his rapt mood
There's no retreat his spirit cannot fill,
No distant leagues, no present, and no past,
No essence that his need may not distil,
All pressed into his service, but he knows
Only the immediate care, if that be good;
The little focus that his words enclose;
As the poor joiner, working at his wood,
Knew not the tree from which the planks were taken,
Knew not the glade from which the trunk was brought,
Knew not the soil in which the roots were fast,
Nor by what centuries of gales the boughs were shaken,
But holds them all beneath his hands at last.

Much goes to little making,—law and skill,   *Craftsmen*
Tradition's usage, each man's separate gift;
Till the slow worker sees that he has wrought
More than he knew of builded truth,
As one who slips through years of youth,
Leaving his young indignant rage,
And finds the years' insensible drift
Brings him achievement with the truce of age.

AUTUMN

Hᴏᴡ sʟᴏᴡ the darkness comes, once daylight's gone,
A slowness natural after English day,
So unimpassioned, tardy to move on,
No southern violence that burns away,
Ardent to live, and eager to be done.
The twilight lingers, etching tree on sky;
The gap's a portal on the ridge's crest;
The partridge coveys call beyond the rye;
Still some red bar of sunset cracks the west;
The orange harvest-moon like a dull sun
Rolls silent up the east above the hill;
Earth like a sleeper breathes, and all is still
This hour of after-day, the dying day's bequest,
This autumn dusk, when neither day nor night
Urges a man to strive or sleep; he stands
Filled with the calm of that familiar place,

Angelus	Idle the shaft beneath his folded hands,
	He who must work the lowlands of his farm,
	Making tenacity his only creed,
	Taking of death and birth his daily need,
	Viewing mortality without alarm.
Autumn	But brief, but short, this hour of quietude
	Gives pause to labour; but a breathing-space
	Granted, before necessity renewed
	Twists up the sinews of his fortitude;

For now the year draws on towards its ending.
Squirrel has hoarded all his nuts, and man,
(Laying for yet another spring his plan,)
Counts over what he has for winter's spending.
Granary's full with heaped and dusty store:
Apples on attic floor
Throughout the house their brackish smell are sending;
The steepled ricks with frost are hoar
In silent yard, the harvest's at its sleeping;
That's slumber now, which once was heyday reaping.
Now retrospect and prospect have their share,
For autumn like the Janus of the year
Holds spring to spring in double-handed keeping.
That sleeps, which once was live; but in the womb
Newly conceived, as corn within the ear,
Another sowing ripens to its bloom.
Further you may not know, but only this:
Nature's an enemy who calls no armistice.
Mistrust the seeming truce, that in the pyre
Of distant woods, and in the gardens' fire,
In pheasants running bronze on furrowed mould,
Burnishes autumn with a coat of gold.
Therefore towards the stubble turn your plough;
Cut gashes new across the healing earth;
Spare not your servant, since to man austere
No respite comes, but bend beneath your vow
Reluctant fields, and bring new life to birth.

Ploughing	Homer and Hesiod and Virgil knew
	The ploughshare in its reasonable shape,

Classical from the moment it was new,   *Ploughing*
Sprung ready-armed, ordained without escape,
And never bettered though man's cunning grew,
And barbarous countries joined the classic reach:
Coulter and swingletree and share and haft
Frugal of ornament as peasants' speech,
Strong to their use and simple as their craft,
Whether to turn the ridge or cleave the rean.
And as the slow Egyptian turns the dark
Loam in his narrow valley where the green
Draws the rich record of the river's mark,
Or as the Mede across his Asian plain,
Watched by the circling mountains topped with snow,
Scores the poor furrow for his meagre wheat
With wooden yoke and lurching buffalo
Pricked by the lazy goad,
And leaves his sowing to the care of God
And takes the southern road
To summer pastures, where the waters flow,
Driving his train of ponies roughly shod
And camels with grave bells, that surly go
Where immemorial caravans have trod,
Marking the trackway with their whitened bones,
His four-span waggons with their homely load,
Black curly lambs that scramble on the stones,
Startling the cricket and the crested lark,
And after summer northward moves again
To reap his harvest in the wickering heat,—
So set your English share, that as a lover tills
The breaking field, and let the blade be keen;
Brace up your hames that collars may not irk,
And urge your horses to the guiding drills,
But knot your hempen reins, and only yerk
Your team by voice, for they must strain
Against a fitful soil, and nobler work
Spared the impatient checking of the rein.
Ploughing's begun among the gentle hills;
Wide skies where cloudy cities travel white
Canopy little acres; in the blanched serene
Tent of the heaven wheel the untidy rooks,

75

Ploughing And settle, gawky, on the browning tracks,
          While man and horse pursue their ancient rite.

Threshing Carted away are all the leaning stooks,
          And from the stackyard comes the thresher's purr.
          England's a humming hive till threshing's done
          And chaff-motes blowing from the emptied sacks
          Mellow the barn in beams of dusty sun.
          Threshing's a game which sets the farm astir
          On fine October mornings when the mist
          Melts to reveal between the steaming stacks
          The thresher lumbering slowly up the lane.
          The gang swarms out in jolly morning vein;
          Unricker, leather strap about his wrist,
          Sackman, and stacker, and the loutish hands,
          And dairymaid agreeable to be kissed,
          And farmer's wife, come out to see the fun
          After a week of baking loaf and pie,
          Admires the young men with a roguish eye;
          And barn-door hens that pick among the grain
          And terrier nosing round for rats, and bands
          Of children, rather shy.
          Straw, chaff, and grain, once work's begun,
          Clean winnowed, sorted fine,
          Heap in appointed place, all rising swift,
          And prudent farmer measures out his thrift,
          And takes his sacks, and thankful sets them by,
          Each fat and solid as a new-killed swine,
          Till they may fill his boarded granary.

Hedging And other cares in autumn fill the days,
and   The care of gardens and of roadside ways.
Ditching The weazened hedger with his hook and stick,
          Brown as a root himself, and stoutly gloved,
          Brishes the hedges, shaving countryside
          Like a cropped schoolboy; brambles, and the loved
          Dog-rose, with hazel-shoots and thorny quick
          Shrivel to bonfire heaps along the waste
          From Michaelmas to Hallowtide
          That hedges be more closely interlaced

Without a gap or flaw   *Hedging*
Next spring in chequered England, growing thick   *and*
Against young stock or colts, for mark the law: *Ditching*
If cattle stray and browse on neighbours' ground,
You may go seek them in the common pound.

And gardener, let your spud be sharp to ridge   *Gardener*
The loam from spiny hedge to hedge;
Labour within your garden square
Till back be broke and light grow rare,
But never heed the sinews' pain
If you may snatch before the rain
Crisp days when clods will turn up rough;
Gentleman robin brown as snuff
With spindle legs and bright round eye
Shall be your autumn company.
Trench deep; dig in the rotting weeds;
Slash down the thistle's greybeard seeds;
Then make the frost your servant; make
His million fingers pry and break
The clods by glittering midnight stealth
Into the necessary tilth.
Then may you shoulder spade and hoe,
And heavy-booted homeward go,
For no new flowers shall be born
Save hellebore on Christmas morn,
And bare gold jasmine on the wall,
And violets, and soon the small
Blue netted iris, like a cry
Startling the sloth of February.

And what of the woodman and his livelihood?   *Woodcraft*
Once in ten years the woodman with his axe
Felling slim undergrowth from stubby boles,
Shall bare the auburn flooring of the copse,
Its ridges, and the sandy rabbit-holes.
Then shall he pare the twigs, and set in stacks
His tall young ash and stripling chestnut poles
That presently shall serve the wreathing hops,
And he shall peel the bark of shorter wood

77

Woodcraft

Clean as a cat in pattens, smelling good,
And sharpen to a point for stakes and spiles,
The whittled slivers flying as he chops,
And lash the shaven wood in ready piles.

But in late autumn with his ropes and guys
He'll go along the peaty forest-tracks
To seek the nobler prize
Blazed with the timber-master's scarlet mark.
Oak will he fell in spring, to gain the bark,
But ash and elm in winter, and the beech
In the short daylight of November thrown,
By Christmas shall lie open, fair to bleach,
As white and hard as bone.
The smoke coils blue above the little camp;
There, in the clearing at the fourfold wents,
On mould of leaves forgotten, reeking, damp
And heavy with autumnal redolence,
Leviathan lies prone.
Bare as the royal antlers of a stag,
His branches fork, and strive to scorn the ground,
Being born for heaven and for heaven crowned,
But man to dust and trees to timber fall,
And comes the hearse or comes the timber-wain
With nut-brown team, patient to stand or haul,
And like a naked savage bound in chain,
With limbs once proud that now through ordure drag,
A captive moves upon his way in thrall;
And that live spirit that once lit the tree,
Fled as a bird when first the ruin came,
Sees only death, defeat, and consequent shame,
Great dignity become a husk; as we
Looking upon the dead demand in vain
Some future use for such mortality;
But being as gods to fallen trees, we know
The lowly uses not within their ken,
Re-fashioning their form to live again,
A humble phoenix stripped of memory.

Their past is sure,

Those woods deep-rooted in the swirl of time,   *Woodcraft*
Temples of myth and piety and fear,
Lovely, obscure;
Dark was the ilex in the Grecian vales,
Crooked the olive, murmurous the lime.
No woodsman but had heard the Dryad cry,
No girl but knew the goat-foot faun was nigh,
And saw the satyr through the branches leer,
And fled from those too-peopled solitudes
Into the open fields of maize and rye.
And women still have memories of woods,
Older than any personal memories;
Writhen, primeval roots, though heads be fair,
Like trees that fan the air with delicacies,
With leaves and birds among the upper air,
High, lifted canopies,
Green and black fingers of the trees, dividing
And reaching out towards an otherwhere,
Threaded with birds and birds' sweet sudden gliding
Pattern and jargoning of tree-tops, such a world
Tangled and resonant and earth-deriding,
Now with the rain-drops' rounded globes bepearled,
And little sullen moons of mistletoe,
Now fretted with the sun, when foxes play
At fables on the dun and foxlike ground
Between the tree-trunks, and the squirrels go
Scuttering with a beechnut newly found,
To vex the pigeon and to scare the jay.

Of such a tall and airy world are they,
Women and woods, with shadowed aisles profound
That none explore.
—Birches, frail whispering company, are these?
Or lovely women rooted into trees?
Daughters of Norsemen, on a foreign shore
Left hostage, while the galley draws away,
Beating its rise and fall on manifold oar,
Beating a pathway to the broken coasts,
Forgetful of its ghosts?

Woodcraft

There is a kinship: down the open ride
She strays, eternal nymph, and glances swift
Into the ambushed depths on either side;
Now fears the shadows, now the rift,
Now fears the silence, now the rustling leaf
That like a footfall with a nearing stride
Startles the stronghold of her unbelief.
Woods are her enemies, yet once she went
Fleeing before a god, and, all but spent,
Slipped from his arms, herself become a tree.
She has forgotten; wood's an enemy;
She has no knowledge of the woodland tracks,
Only a knowledge of her jeopardy.
And with lost steps, neglectful of her pride,
Stumbles towards the music of the axe.
There, brown old sylvan god, the woodsman plies
His craft and drives his wedge,
Spitting to ease the rub of tool on hands,
And she arrested at the clearing's edge
Awakened stands,
With panic terror fading from her eyes.

Autumn

Now I have told the year from dawn to dusk,
Its morning and its evening and its noon;
Once round the sun our slanting orbit rolled,
Four times the seasons changed, thirteen the moon;
Corn grew from seed to husk,
The young spring grass to fodder for the herds;
Drought came, and earth was grateful for the rain;
The bees streamed in and out the summer hives;
Birds wildly sang; were silent; birds
With summer's passing fitfully sang again;
The loaded waggon crossed the field; the sea
Spread her great generous pasture as a robe
Whereon the slow ships, circling statelily,
Are patterned round the globe.
The ample busyness of life went by,
All the full busyness of lives
Unknown to fame, made lovely by no words:
The shepherd lonely in the winter fold;

The tiller following the eternal plough   *Autumn*
Beneath a stormy or a gentle sky;
The sower with his gesture like a gift
Walking the furrowed hill from base to brow;
The reaper in the piety of thrift
Binding the sheaf against his slanted thigh.

And lastly,—since it was of Kent I told,   *Orchards*
Kent, and the parcels of her acreage,—
Peculiar autumn crops
Leave one thing more to tell,
Spilt from the horn of plenty to my page,
Spicing my line with tart or resinous smell.
Apples and hops made Kent's clean autumn wine,
Orchard and garden, loaded, looped with swags,
Scarlet and green, on bough and bine;
Heavy as apples, say we, light as hops,
Where the leafy awning sags,
And weighted boughs are crutched on forkèd props.

I told in spring of the orchard's enemies,
Wrapped in cocoon or pert upon the wing,
And of the care that prudent growers bring,
But now the swoln fulfilment of the trees,
Coloured and round,
Demands another order: nimble boys,
Reared ladders, bushel baskets on the ground,
And pick, pick, pick, while days are calm and fine.
These orchards that have lonely stood since spring,
Swelling their fruit unnoted in the sun,
Are populous suddenly, with ringing voice,
September mornings, when the sun's yet low,
And dew upon the leas
Makes brambles glisten and the mushrooms grow.
Codlin's already stripped; his day was done
When August holidays were first begun,
Being the children's apple, earliest ripe
And nothing worth for keeping; only worth
Young teeth, and summer fun.
But quarrendens, and russets nicely browned,

Orchards
And common Councillors, of varied stripe,
And pippins smelling of the rainy earth
Wait to be harvested
With Peasgood Nonesuch, giant in his girth,
Cox, Blenheim, Ribstone, properly renowned,
Apples that wait for Christmas, darkly stored
On shelf or floor, not touching, one by one.
But by the red cheek never be misled;
For virtue, flavour, seek the acid green,
Of looks less kindly, but of sharp reward
Like stringent wit that keeps a matter keen.

Full carts, full baskets, in the misty sun.
And cider claims the windfall on the sward.

Making
Cider
I saw within the wheelwright's shed
The big round cartwheels, blue and red;
A plough with blunted share;
A blue tin jug; a broken chair;
And paint in trial patchwork square
Slapped up against the wall;
The lumber of the wheelwright's trade,
And tools on benches neatly laid,
The brace, the adze, the awl;

And, framed within the latticed panes,
Above the cluttered sill,
Saw rooks upon the stubble hill
Seeking forgotten grains;

And all the air was sweet and shrill
With juice of apples heaped in skips,
Fermenting, rotten, soft with bruise,
And all the yard was strewn with pips,
Discarded pulp, and wrung-out ooze
That ducks with rummaging flat bill
Searched through beside the cider-press
To gobble in their greediness.

The young men strained upon the crank
To wring the last reluctant inch.

They laughed together, fair and frank,
And threw their loins across the winch.

Making
Cider

A holiday from field and dung,
From plough and harrow, scythe and spade,
To dabble in another trade,
To crush the pippins in the slats,
And see that in the little vats
An extra pint was wrung;
While round about the worthies stood,
Profuse in comment, praise or blame,
Content the press should be of wood,
Advising rum, decrying wheat,
And black strong sugar makes it sweet,
But still resolved, with maundering tongue,
That cider could not be the same
As once when they were young;
But still the young contemptuous men
Laughed kindly at their old conceit,
And strained upon the crank again.

Now barrels ranged in portly line

Making
Cider

Mature through winter's sleep,
Aping the leisured sloth of wine
That dreams by Tiber or by Rhine,
Mellowing slow and deep;
But keen and cold the northern nights
Sharpen the quiet yard,
And sharp like no rich southern wine
The tang of cider bites;
For here the splintered stars and hard
Hold England in a frosty guard,
Orion and the Pleiades
Above the wheelwright's shed,
And Sirius resting on the trees
While all the village snores abed.

Hop
Garden

Hops ripen to their picking. Down the rows
Of pickers by their tally-baskets bent,
The gaitered master goes,
Slapping his leggings with a hazel switch,
Nodding good-day to folk he knows,
From London slums poured yearly into Kent,
Waking the province with their cockney slang,
And feathered hats, and fear of showers;
Down leafy tunnels, dappled by the sun,
Down sea-green aisles, where loam is brown and rich
Between the hills, and overhead the flowers
In pale imponderable clusters hang,
He loiters, followed by his spaniel bitch
Close in to heel, sulky for lack of gun.
Passed from his keeping now, those bines
That since their earliest shooting had his care;
Already severed, half the lines
Are fallen withered, and the poles are bare,
But in the tallies rise the soft green heaps,
High, and are emptied, once again to fill,
For carts between the garden and the kiln
Slow but unceasing ply,
And down the trampled lane come for a fresh supply.

Oast

Dusk sends the pickers home to camp,

But the country works while London sleeps.　　　*Oast*
Within the oast the sulphurous furnace roars;
Men shovel coal, and clang the doors,
And in an inner room play cards and dice
Beneath a smoking lamp;
Swear; spit; and grumble at the crop, the price,
The master's profit and the labourer's wage
With a fictitious indignation; rage
Born of sound understanding, sprung
Like lovers' quarrels from a prickly tongue,
Vain of its independence and its wit,
With hearts belying speech,
Each against foreigner defending each,
But bitter among friends,—unspoken laws.
Comes here the master: silence falls.
Shadows of men on whitewashed walls
Throw dice; deal cards; turn down the lamp; puff smoke;
Rise up; and on a sudden redly lit
Pass to the kiln like demons; fiercely stoke;
And to the inner room return to swear and spit,
To gamble and to grumble, spit and swear.
But he, the master climbs the ladder-stair
To the upper loft, where silence and pale peace
Hold volatile lease;
The upper loft, where mountains on the floor
Of sapless flowers, sap-robbed flowers, swell
Bulky and weightless, ashen as fair hair
Beneath a lamp, ashen as moonlit corn,
As stubble newly shorn,
Hops dried and ready for the rhythmic press
Crushing their levity to a nothingness
Of prosy tonnage scribbled on a slate,
—Those airy mountains packed in terms of weight;—
The press that whirls its shadow on the bare
White wall and raftered ceiling, wheel and spoke
Distorted, laying like a heavier cloak
New burdens of resin on the loaded air.

Now the old drier shuffles across the loft,
Opens the oast-house door,

Oast   Where hops spread drying, sappy, green, and soft,
Wreathed with the mounting of the faint blue smoke
In a round chamber with a pointed roof,
And the scent overpowers.
Knee-deep he slouches, kicking up the flowers;
Like an old priest at some clandestine rite
Round the white walls, he, dressed in white,
Stealthily travels, ancient and aloof.
Ancient as man on earth, man turns to wine
Or bread earth's produce; seeks escape or need;
Release, necessity, the alternating creed;
Necessity, release; food, anodyne.
So the old drier, forty or fifty years,
Kicks up the hops, that they be evenly dried
Each autumn as the harvest comes again,
Grown old at a lonely task; he hears
The sound of voices in the yard outside,
The clang of furnace doors, the tread of men;
And they, as they swing homeward down the lane,
Look back at the oast and the single lighted pane
Like a square beacon yellow in the night,
And know that the drier slouches round the wall.

Vintage   Yet I recall
Another harvest, not beneath this sky
So Saxon-fair, so washed by dews and rain;
Another harvest, where the gods still rouse,
And stretch, and waken with the evenfall.
Down from the hill the slow white oxen crawl,
Dragging the purple waggon heaped with must,
Raising on sundered hoofs small puffs of dust,
With scarlet tassels on their milky brows,
Gentle as evening moths. Beneath the yoke
Lounging against the shaft they fitful strain
To draw the waggon on its creaking spoke,
And all the vineyard folk
With staves and shouldered tools surround the wain.
The wooden shovels take the purple stain,
The dusk is heavy with the wine's warm load;
Here the long sense of classic measure cures

The spirit weary of its difficult pain;   *Vintage*
Here the old Bacchic piety endures,
Here the sweet legends of the world remain.
Homeric waggons lumbering the road;
Virgilian litanies among the bine;
Pastoral sloth of flocks beneath the pine;
The swineherd watching, propped upon his goad,
Under the chestnut trees the rootling swine.
Who could so stand, and see this evening fall,
This calm of husbandry, this redolent tilth,
This terracing of hills, this vintage wealth,
Without the pagan sanity of blood
Mounting his veins in young and tempered health?
Who could so stand, and watch processional
The vintners, herds, and flocks in dusty train
Wend through the molten evening to regain
The terraced farm and trodden threshing-floor
Where late the flail
Tossed high the maize in scud of gritty ore,
And lies half-buried in the heap of grain,—
Who could so watch, and not forget the rack
Of wills worn thin and thought become too frail,
Nor roll the centuries back
And feel the sinews of his soul grow hale,
And know himself for Rome's inheritor?

O Mantuan! that sang the bees and vines,
The tillage and the flocks,
I saw the round moon rise above the pines,
One quiet planet prick the greening west,
As goats came leaping up the stony crest
And the crook'd goatherd moved between the rocks.
That moon, that star, above my English weald,
Hung at that hour, and I not there to see;
Shining through mist above the dew-drenched field,
Making a cavern of the plumy tree.
Then all my deep acquaintance with that land,
Crying for words, welled up; as man who knows
That Nature, tender enemy, harsh friend,
Takes from him soon the little that she gave,

Vintage   Yet for his span will labour to defend
His courage, that his soul be not a slave,
Whether on waxen tablet or on loam,
Whether with stylus or with share and heft
The record of his passage he engrave,
And still, in toil, takes heart to love the rose.

Then thought I, Virgil! how from Mantua reft,
Shy as a peasant in the courts of Rome,
You took the waxen tablets in your hand,
And out of anger cut calm tales of home.

Isfahan, April 1926

THE
GARDEN

DEDICATION
TO
KATHERINE DRUMMOND

How well I know what I mean to do
When the sweet moist days of Autumn come:
Clear my garden of wicked weeds
And write a poem to give to you.

A long, rank poem of autumn words,
Looking over the summer and spring.
My age is autumn, and yours is—what?
Winter? ah no, that's another thing.

Yours is the year that counts no season;
I can never be sure what age you are.
A girl in her running moods, no reason?
A woman of wisdom crepuscular?

Lover of words for their English beauty,
Lover of friends for their tested bond,
(Oh faithful tolerant heart, so rare
In visions of virtue, seen beyond!
Seen beyond cheapness, seen beyond meanness,
Meagre estimates not in your score.
Credit the others, make yourself debtor,
Lest in the total you might poll more!)

Lover of woods, of words, of flowers,
Lover yourself of the things I love,
Friendship was made of the quiet hours
Hung between earth and the sky above.

Flowers and clouds and the last unknown,
All in your garden or soft deep room
Where peace obtained and the window showed
On a twilight gloom that was not gloom.

You loved me too, as I like to think;
I felt your love as a benediction
In tranquil branches above me spread,
Over my sometimes troubled head,
A cedar of Lebanon, dark as ink,
And grave as a valediction.

You are the wise, the brave, the gentle;
The rivulets of my many moods
Flowed unchecked by your quiet chair
As the freshet flows through the watching woods.

Ah, could I tell you, ah, could I give you
Half of the strength you have given to me!
Half of a garden, half of a poem,
Then would the rivulet run to the sea.

But how well I know what I really do
When St. Martin's golden Summer comes:

I pull no weed from my garden slums
And write no poem that's fit for you.

Hide in the woods instead, and dream
As the beeches turn to their autumn brown
And acorns plop in the swollen stream;
Sit on a rotting log; scrawl down
Rubbish of verses fit for fire,
Gardener, poet, on single pyre,
Liberal, losel, catching the last
Chance of the mothlike summer past,—
Winter's ahead, and our days are few.

Failing as gardener, failing as poet,
Giving so little to all I love,
What have I done with my life as I know it,
A shortening beat on a short patrol?

How to detect the advance of age,
The growth of the moss on the hoary soul,
The loss of the generous early rage,
The drab of hoping no more from life,
Which marks the transit from youth to sage?

What did we ever expect from life?
Fame? adventure? a tranquil bliss?
Ah no, it was never those varied things,
The stocks that soar or the lark that sings;
It was the ardour that lit the whole,
Not expectation of that or this.

Age is the loss of that early zest;
The onset of age is the flame gone low;
Signs of the end, of the deathly rest
Sought in the pianissimo
By a heart gone weak and a spirit tired
From the long delusion of things desired.

That is an age which has laid no touch
On your silver hair or your laughing eyes;
Tarnished you not with sardonic smutch,
For your heart is young though it may be wi
And your spirit is still intuitive.

So take the little I have to give,
Here in a poem to fill your leisure
Where every word is lived and true.
The weeds in my garden remain as green,
And I cannot tell if I bring you pleasure,
But the little patch I have cleared for you,
That one small patch of my soul is clean.

THE GARDEN

S MALL PLEASURES must correct great tragedies,
Therefore of gardens in the midst of war
I boldly tell. Once of the noble land
I dared to pull the organ-stops, the deep
Notes of the bass, the diapason's range
Of rich rotation, yielding crop by crop;
Of season after season as the wheel
Turned cyclic in the grooves and groves of time;
I told the classic tools, the plough, the scythe,
In husbandry's important ritual,
But now of agriculture's little brother
I touch the pretty treble, pluck the string,
Making the necklace of a gardener's year,
A gardener's job, for better or for worse
Strung all too easily in beads of verse.
No strong, no ruthless plough-share cutting clods,
No harrow toothéd as the saurian jaws,
Shall tear or comb my sward of garden theme,
But smaller spade and hoe and lowly trowel
And ungloved fingers with their certain touch.

(Delicate are the tools of gardener's craft,
Like a fine woman next a ploughboy set,
But none more delicate than gloveless hand,
That roaming lover of the potting-shed,
That lover soft and tentative, that lover
Desired and seldom found, green-fingered lover

Who scorned to take a woman to his bed.)
So to such small occasions am I fallen,
And in the midst of war,
(Heroic days, when all the pocket folk
Were grabbed and shaken by a larger hand
And lived as they had never lived before
Upon a plane they could not understand
And gasping breathed an atmosphere too rare,
But took it quickly as their native air,
Such big events
That from the slowly opening fount of time
Dripped from the leaky faucet of our days,)
I tried to hold the courage of my ways
In that which might endure,
Daring to find a world in a lost world,
A little world, a little perfect world,
With owlet vision in a blinding time,
And wrote and thought and spoke
These lines, these modest lines, almost demure,
What time the corn still stood in sheaves,
What time the oak
Renewed the million dapple of her leaves.

Yet shall the garden with the state of war
Aptly contrast, a miniature endeavour
To hold the graces and the courtesies
Against a horrid wilderness. The civil
Ever opposed the rude, as centuries'
Slow progress laboured forward, then the check,
Then the slow uphill climb again, the slide
Back to the pit, the climb out of the pit,
Advance, relapse, advance, relapse, advance,
Regular as the measure of a dance;
So does the gardener in little way
Maintain the bastion of his opposition
And by a symbol Keep civility;
So does the brave man strive
To keep enjoyment in his breast alive
When all is dark and even in the heart
Of beauty feeds the pallid worm of death.

Much toil, much care, much love and many years
Went to the slow reward; a grudging soil
Enriched or lightened following its needs:
Potash and compost, stable-dung, blood, bones,
Spent hops in jade-green sacks, the auburn leaves
Rotted and rich, the wood-ash from the hearth
For sticky clay; all to a second use
Turned in a natural economy,
And many a robin perched on many a sod
Watched double-trenching for his benefit
Through the companionable russet days,
But only knew the digger turned to worm
For him, and had no foresight of the frost
Later to serve the digger and his clod
Through winter months, for limitations rule
Robins and men about their worms and wars,
The robin's territory; and man's God.

But the good gardener with eyes on ground
(Lifted towards the sunset as he scrapes
His tools at day's end, looks into the west,
Examining the calm or angry sky
To reckon next day's chance of fair or ill,
Of labour or of idleness enforced,)
Sees only what he sees, oh happy he!
Makes his small plot his arbiter, his bourn,
Being too lightly built to suffer pain
That's unremitting, pain of broken love,
Or pain of war that tears too red a hole.
He will endure his trials willy-nilly,
The plaguy wind, the cold, the drought, the rain,
All, to his mind, ill-timed and in excess,
But finds a sanctuary. He knows, he knows
The disappointments, the discomfitures,
The waste, the dash of hopes, the sweet surprise
Sprung in forgotten corner; knows the loss,
Attempts defeated, optimism balked;
He may not pause to lean upon his spade,
And even in the interruption brought
By friends, he will not stroll

At simple ease, but ever dart his eyes
Noticing faults, and feeling fingers twitch,
Eager to cut, to tie, correct, promote,
Sees all shortcomings with the stranger's eye,
An absent-minded host with inward fret,
The most dissatisfied of men, whose hope
Outran achievement and is leading yet.

(Still there are moments when the shadows fall
And the low sea of flowers, wave on wave,
Spreads to the pathway from the rosy wall
Saying in coloured silence, "Take our all;
You gave to us, and back to you we gave.

"You dreamed us, and we made your dream come true.
We are your vision, here made manifest.
You sowed us, and obediently we grew,
But, sowing us, you sowed more than you knew
And something not ourselves has done the rest.")

Unlike the husbandman who sets his field
And knows his reckoned crop will come to birth
Varying but a little in its yield
After the necessary months ensealed
Within the good the generative earth,

The gardener half artist must depend
On that slight chance, that touch beyond control
Which all his paper planning will transcend;
He knows his means but cannot rule his end;
He makes the body: who supplies the soul?

Sometimes, as poet feels his pencil held,
Sculptor his chisel cutting effortless,
Painter his brush behind his grasp impelled,
Unerring guidance, theory excelled,
When rare Perfection gives a rounded Yes,

So does some magic in his humbler sphere,
Some trick of Nature, slant of curious light,

Some grouped proportion, splendid or severe
In feast of Summer or the Winter sere,
Show the designer one thing wholly right.

Music from notes and poetry from verse
Grow to a consummation rare, entire,
When harmony resolves without disperse
The broken pattern of the universe
And joins the particles of our desire.

Hint of the secret synthesis that lies
So surely round some corner of our road;
That deepest canon of our faith, the prize
We look for but shall never realise;
Suspected cipher that implies a code.

Rosetta Stone of beauty come by chance
Into the testing hands of gardener's loves,
Rich hieroglyphic of significance
Only denied to our poor ignorance.
—Those orchards of Rosetta and their doves!

Should we resolve the puzzle, lose the zest,
Should we once know our last our full intent,
If all were staringly made manifest,
The mystery and the elusive quest,
Then less than ever should we be content.

The Morning Glory climbs towards the sun
As we by nature sadly born to strive
And our unending race of search to run,
Forever started, never to be won,
—And might be disappointed to arrive.

WINTER

BLACKOUT.

Quiet. The tick of clock
Shall bring you peace,
To your uncertain soul
Give slow increase.

The blackened windows shut
This inward room
Where you may be alone
As in the tomb.

A tomb of life not death,
Life inward, true,
Where the world vanishes
And you are you.

War brings this seal of peace,
This queer exclusion,
This novel solitude,
This rare illusion,

As to the private heart
All separate pain
Brings loss of friendly light
But deeper, darker gain.

97

Not only war, but natural Winter carries
This valuable and enforced retreat,
As monks will seek in contemplation's cell
An increment of quiet holiness,
Prolonged novena,—so the Winter gives
A blameless idleness to active hands
And liberates the vision of the soul.
Darkness is greater light, to those who see;
Solitude greater company to those
Who hear the immaterial voices; those
Who dare to be alone.

Yet there are days when courage, hardly pressed,
Staggers to meet the unaccountable foe
More dangerous than known danger; days when cold
Frightens with lack of mercy, days when sleet
Blinds as an evil and obscuring thing,
The very enemy of sight and light,
A force iniquitous, an infamy
Whose only lust is ruin; days when murk
Darkens before the clock's expected hour
And blows the little taper of our cheer;
Days when the wind, which once was summer breeze,
Rips through the canvas of the air, with fangs
Savaging the poor shelter of our house;
Days when our gentle and habitual friends
The trees, the roads, take part in enmity,
Trees twisting roots that in the summer held
The reading schoolboy in their hammock slung
Over the stream, but now like pythons wreathe
Waiting to rack new sons of Laocoon;
When lanes that led us to the lighted pane
Now in their frozen malice make us fall;
When the mild hills that big as guardians stood
Watching our valley, take another shape
Or hide themselves entire, so we, not seeing
But knowing only that they still are there,
Wonder what transformation huge and bad
Corrupts them in their cloud, and in our awe
Cower, and push our fearful thought away.

It is not Winter, not the cold we fear;
It is the dreadful echo of our void,
The malice all around us, manifest;
Loud-mouthed interpreter of constant whispers
Mostly ignored, or drowned within the song
Of cheerfulness and shallow disregard.
The athletic spirit, like a shouting boy,
Leaps to all reassurance, shuns the dour
Disquiet plucking mutely at his sleeve,
And seeks the climate native to his mind
Where day suffices day, but even he
When lowering Nature grips, must vacillate
Disconsolate before the frightful day
With a strange wonder and a strange alarm.

No natural dread, no dread of age or death,
—Tractable phantoms do they both appear—
But an unmanageable intimation
Arousing with an apprehended call
That rabble in the basement of our being,
Ragged and gaunt, that seldom rush to light
But in a cellar with the scurrying rats
Live out their bleached existence till the cry
Whistles them up the stairs, the curs, the beggars,
And sets them running in a pack released
To chase the frightened rabbit of the soul.

Not always thus, for the resilient heart
Thankfully lifts, the richer for that hour.
Let but one gleam and promise of the sun
Redly dissolve the mist, unfreeze the lane
And put some colour back where there was none,
Then in our pathos do we lift our eyes
And tread with confidence our usual path
Fearing no treachery; then we behold
Beauty return with colour and with shape,
(As beauty, for completeness, must observe.)

Then will the fine-drawn branches of the Winter
Stretch fingers of a lean but generous hand

THE GARDEN

Against a morning sky of cloud where mingle
Doves and flamingoes, over pented roofs
Of clustered homestead with its barns and lichen
Green in the rain but golden in the sun;
The great red threshing engine standing ready
Out in the stack-yard, and the green tarpaulin
Tossed as a tent above the waiting ricks,
So viridescent, it repeats the lichen;
The cottages repeating all the apples
That ever hung with cheeks towards the sun.

Quiet you down, you troubled soul; lie down
As patient dog when bidden, in a corner;
Forget those days when you could not control
Something that rose unbidden and unknown.
Seize on your comfort when you may; resume
The little things that match your little scheme,
And, as you travel on your country road
And see the bonfire blazing from the brish
To match the sunrise scarlet in the sky
With smoke as full and blue as plumes of swan,
(Since white is blue in shadow), leave your fear,
Let the brief terror go, and turn again
To the more comfortable daily rule.

. . . As once in childhood, when the creep of dusk
Peopled the hedges with a breed of shapes,
And pollard willows turned to knarly apes,
The hollies to a host of men in capes,
And whitened birch-pole to a sharpened tusk,

The stump of chestnut to a manikin,
The tufted elm to an advancing bear,
The very ditch to some unseemly lair,
—Then, when a lighted window showed its square,
A sudden token of the peace within,

The room we knew, security entire,
Leapt as a picture, self-contained, complete,
A sanctuary to our running feet,
A box of walls, a rational retreat,

But most of all the warm, the fendered fire,

The fire our friend, that symbol since the cave,
Which on a wintry morning, still half-dark,
In roadside fireside when our days are stark
But bonfire brishings of the hedges spark,
Touches our childish heart, and makes us brave.

Winter. What's Winter? Is it cowardly
To draw the curtain on the misery
Of outward day? shut out the tears of rain
And wind-dishevelled ancient hair of trees
And soakèd garden seen through window-pane?
Oh no! for here a different pleasure offers;
Here may we dream of different beauty seen,
Desired though not fulfilled, that final beauty
Denied to all our scheming as we know
Too well, yet still delude ourselves in vision
Unreasonable, in pathetic faith
As the advancing soul, abashed, disheartened,
Loses itself in night to reach a day
Resplendent after darkness,—so in Winter
The gardener sees what he will never see.

Here, in his lamp-lit parable, he'll scan
Catalogues bright with colour and with hope,
Dearest delusions of creative mind,
His lamp-lit walls, his lamp-lit table painting
Fabulous flowers flung as he desires.
Fantastic, tossed, and all from shilling packet
—An acre sprung from one expended coin,—
Visions of what might be.
                              We dream our dreams.
What should we be, without our fabulous flowers?
The gardener dreams his special own alloy
Of possible and the impossible.

He dreams an orchard neatly pruned and spurred,
Where Cox' Orange jewels with the red
Of Worcester Permain, and the grass beneath

Blows with narcissus and the motley crocus,
Rich as Crivelli, fresh as Angelo
Poliziano, or our English Chaucer
Or Joachim du Bellay, turn by turn.
He dreams again, extravagant, excessive,
Of planted acres most unorthodox
Where Scarlet Oaks would flush our English fields
With passionate colour as the Autumn came,
Quercus coccinea, that torch of flame
Blown sideways as by some Atlantic squall
Between its native north America
And this our moderate island. Or again
He dreams of forests made of flow'ring trees
Acre on acre, thousands in their pride,
Cherry and almond, crab and peach and plum,
Not like their working cousins grown for use
But in an arrant spendthrift swagger cloak
Squandered across th' astonished countryside.

What woodlands here! No beech, no sycamore,
No rutted chestnut, no, nor wealden oak,
Trunks rising straight from sun-shot, shade-flecked
    ground,
Elephants' legs, set gray and solid-round,
No green-brown distance of the mossy ride,
But tossing surf of blossom, frothy heads,
Lather of rose, of cream, of ice-green white,
Vapour and spindrift blown upon the air,
Scudding down rides and avenues more fair
Even than usual woodlands in the Spring
Or at the Summer's height;
(That's saying much, God knows; though saying only
A truth to him who through the woodland goes
Rapt, but aware; alone yet never lonely;
And all the changes of their movement knows.)

Oh these imagined woods in a clear treble
Pure as a boy's voice, purer than a woman's,
With coral deepening those high, light notes
Of white and pink and rose and palest yellow:

They are more lovely than known loveliness,
They are the consummation of a vision
Seen by rare travellers on Tibetan hills
—Bitter escarpments cut by knives of wind,
Eaves of the world, the frightful lonely mountains,—
Or in Yunnan and Sikkim and Nepal
Or Andes ranges, over all this globe
Giant in travelled detail, dwarf on maps;
Forrest and Farrer, Fortune, Kingdon-Ward,
Men that adventured in the lost old valleys,
Difficult, dangerous, or up the heights,
Tired and fevered, blistered, hungry, thin,
But drunk enough to set a house on fire
When the last moment of their worthless quest
Startled them with reward, a flash as sudden
As the king-fisher's blue on English stream.

(They say, such travellers were suspect there
Where none would come for other quest than gold
Or trade, that other token form of gold.
Gold may mean different things to different men.
To one man, it could mean the Golden Bell,
Forsythia suspensa, hanging yellow
Along bare branches, such a natural gold
Paying no dividend, as in our cold
Dark February, alien golden bells
Deepen our pale young sunlight, gild our frost,
Since that lone raider rang his useless bells of gold.)

And this, in these invented woods, may take
The place of underwood, replace the tall
Thirteen-year chestnut, fit for poles and spiles;
Here is romance, in this imagined forest,
These different rides of laylock and Forsythia;
Azalea in a peaty soil; magnolia
Cupping its goblets down the narrow aisles;
Vines and solanum wreathing Silver Birches,
Wild waving overhead, to lift the eyes
Surfeited with the wealth on lower level.

Think, and imagine: this might be your truth;
Follow my steps, oh gardener, down these woods.
Luxuriate in this my startling jungle.
I dream, this winter eve. A millionaire
Could plant these forests of a poet's dream.
A poet's dream costs nothing; yet is real.

The gardener sits in lamplight, soberer
Than I who mix such lyrical and wild
Impossibilities with what a sober man
Considers sense. Yet I, poor poet, I
Am likewise a poor practised gardener
Knowing the Yes and better still the No.
Sense must prevail, nor waste extravagant
Such drunken verse on such December dreams.

Yet I do find it difficult indeed
To break away from visions in this drear
Winter of northern island. I must love
The warmer sun and with nostalgia pine
For those my birthright climates on the coast
Mediterranean of southern Spain.

Homesick we are, and always, for another
And different world.
                        And so the traveller
Down the long avenue of memory
Sees in perfection that was never theirs
Gardens he knew, and takes his steps of thought
Down paths that, half-imagined and half-real,
Are wholly lovely with a loveliness
Suffering neither fault, neglect, nor flaw;
By visible hands not tended, but by angels
Or by St. Phocas, gentlest patron saint
Of gardeners. . . . Such wisdom of perfection
Never was ours in fact though ours in faith,
And since we live in fabric of delusion
Faith may well serve a turn in place of fact.

Luxury of escape! In thought he wanders

Down paths now more than paths, down paths once seen.
Gold is their gravel, not the gold that paves
Ambition's highway; velvet is their green;
Blue is the water of the tide that laves
Their island shore where terraces step steep
Down to the unimaginable coves
Where wash on silver sand the secret seas.
Above such coves, such seas, he strays between
Straight cypresses or rounded orange-trees,
And sees a peasant draw a pail from deep
Centennial well; and finds a wealth in these.

Across the landscape of his memory
Bells ring from distant steeples, no cracked bell
Marring the harmony, but all as pure
As that spring-water drawn from that clear well.
What time the English loam is bare and brown
Elsewhere he roams and lets his reason drown
In thought of beauty seen. There was a key
Opened an iron door within the wall
Of the thick ramparts of a fortress town
Where the great mountains sudden and remote
Like clouds at tether rose,
But the near larkspur seemed as tall
Dashing her spire of azure on their snows;
And, wandering, he might recall
Another garden, seen as in a moat
Reflected, green, and white with swans afloat,
Shut in a wood where, mirrored sorrowful,
A marble Muse upon her tablets wrote.

Look, where he strays!
Images, like those slow and curving swans,
Sail sensuous up, and these drab northern days,
This isle of mist, this sun a shield of bronze,
Melt in the intenser light away.

Or, as his vision grows particular
In focus of his lamplight, he may see
Detail of gardens in his little lens,

Bright in their miniature.
Gardens of Persia, where the thin canal
Runs in transparency on turquoise tiles
Down to the lost pavilion, broken, spoilt,
Decaying as the peach and almond wake
Beneath the snow-white mountains when the Spring
Melts snow, and water and the blossom break.

Or he may see the great Escorial,
Barrack fanatical, and smell the box
Hot in the August sun; or pace the strait
Paths of the Generalifë, oddly hitched
To scarps where all the nightingales of Spain
Sing to the moon, or in some dark Italian
Garden find symphonies of leaves and water:
The ilex, and the fountain, and the cool
Nymph dipping marble foot in living pool.

Gardens of the ideal, the sole Kingdom;
All his, attained, possessed, held beyond loss.
Take a prince prisoner and make him yours!
Princely he roves, but with a soft nostalgia
Sweetening half the pain that it embalms,
—As some young simple soldier, far from home,
Goes walks down cottage paths, and speaks no word
Of flowers he perceived or birds he heard,
But holds that corner of his exiled heart
Private for that rare pious pilgrimage
When he with his true self may live apart.

Thus do I love my England, though I roam.
Thus do I love my England: I am hers.
What could be said more simply? As a lover
Says of his mistress, I am hers, she mine,
So do I say of England: I do love her.
She is my shape; her shape my very shape.
Her present is my grief; her past, my past.
Often I rage, resent her moderate cast,
Yet she is mine, I hers, without escape.
The cord of birth annexes me for ever.

And so when long and idle winter dusk
Forces me into lamplight, I must make
Impracticable beauty for my England.

Ah dreams, impracticable dreams! What dreams
Lie buried in that box all gardeners know,
Labels that once belonged to living plants
But now like little tombstones set aside
Rest on a shelf, nor wait another morn.
They're dead; we could not grow them; they are dead;
Dead as a finished love that will not throw
Fresh shoots again beyond that fine first burst
Of love or spring of year.
                                    Small cemetery,
These labels were our hopes; we saw them grow
Into a loveliness we cannot know.
The catalogues misled us, as a poem
Misleads us, or the promises of love;
We heard their music, and as chords they go.

Box of the Dead, these labels sadly pulled
From base of shrivelled plants, yet set aside
For that bright day when death may be replaced
By youngling surging on another tide.

Book of the Dead, that private catalogue
Of hope defeated, list of hope and droop.
Oh what a book is that! a year-by-year
Order from nurserymen, expensive, modest;
The cost meant nothing where the love meant all.

Modest we are in hope, and in defeat
Docile and sad, but still renewed in hope.
What lovely names in that Dead Book survive,
Names that might be the names of those we loved, and died;
Forever dead, and never could revive.

Winter must be the season that induces
Such melancholy, and the heart seduces
Towards a feast of pleasure and of pain;

And I remember once a stranger said,
Trudging about my garden when the snow
Had laid a thin and ugly film, "I know
You think your garden shameful now, and wilt
As this intruder witnesses your guilt,
But I like winter best, for in the plain
Ground where the shortened stalks look dead
I read the labels with a greater ease,
And with the eye of faith
See better life than any life, for these
Who have the look of death."

Oh delicate heart! I never knew your name.

Truth is not wholly truth, that only truth observes.
There is a finer truth that sometimes swerves,
And like reflections in a bandy mirror
Astonishes through very twist of error.

Beauty's not always in a scarlet robe.
She wears an old black shawl;
She flouts the flesh and shows the bone
When winter trees are tall.
More beautiful than fact may be
The shadow on the wall.

Beauty's not always prinked in all her vaunt;
It pleases her to speak
In basic whisper to an ear

That will not find her bleak;
The hearing ear, the seeing eye
Who catch her signs oblique.

Oh, fairer than young harlot Summer proud
This subtle, crooked, wise
Old Winter croaks a different truth
Scorning the sensuous lies;
Etches the finer skeleton
For more perceptive eyes.

The moody seasons with their lift and fall!
A light comes through the mist, and all
Is painted by the great brush of the sun.
He goes behind a cloud, and all is dun.

Strange, yet not passing strange, that our poor mood
(Too finely balanced for a world too crude)
Should suffer shade and sunlight as a wood
Now lit in shafts, now light-less, flat, and stale.

Our mood is Nature's, and ourselves too frail.

Gardener, dwell not long on Book of Dead,
Nor yet on desperate mood beneath the lamp;
Think, rather, of the triumph when you said
"I drained this sodden bed and saved from damp."
These were the long laborious tasks you did;
These are the practical, the small
Pert boasting Jacks against the Giants tall
Of winter trees, as bony and as harsh
As knuckled willows lining Romney Marsh.

But frost will come, and if you well prepare
Your trenching, never taken unaware
By that strange metalled grip
That steals the vigil of your guardianship
And does the second half of work begun
And changes every aspect while the sun
Founders incarnadine, to reappear

Paler with morning, on an earth forlorn
But magical with mystery of mist
When frozen cobwebs hang from frozen thorn
Stiff in their frailty,—then you may rejoice
That at the cost of aching spine and wrist
You took November foresight as your choice
And laid your garden ready as a feast
For frost to finger, and through clods to run.

Frost! Use as friend; forestall as enemy.
A gardener's scrap of wisdom, simply learnt.
Rash maiden growth may be as truly burnt
By chill as fire, to dangle limp and lame.
Young leaves hang seared by frost as though by flame;
See the young tender chestnut in the wood
As though a Goth with torch had passed that way
When the three ice-saints hold their sway
In middle-May:
Saint Boniface, Saint Servais, and the boy
Saint Pancras, martyred long before he came
To manhood, with his fame
Still known to Canterbury in his church,
With legendary power to destroy
Orchards of Kent that wither at his name
At coming of his feast-day with the smirch
Of blossom browned and future apples trim
Lost at the touch of his aberrant whim.

Therefore, lest this inclement friend should maim
Your valued plants, plunge pots within a frame
Sunk deep in sand or ashes to the rim,
Warm nursery when nights and days are grim;
But in the long brown borders were the frost
May hold its mischievous and midnight play
And all your winnings of the months be lost
In one short gamble when the dice are tossed
Finally and forever in few hours,
—The chance your skill, the stake your flowers,—
Throw bracken, never sodden, light and tough
In almost weightless armfuls down, to rest

Buoyant on tender and frost-fearing plants;
Or set the wattled hurdle in a square
Protective, where the north-east wind is gruff,
As sensitive natures seek for comfort lest
Th' assault of life be more than they can bear,
And find an end, not in timidity
But death's decisive certainty.

And think on present task for open days.
November sees your digging, rough and brown,
For frost, that natural harrow,
To break your furrows down;
Your spade-wide spits, laborious turned by hand,
So trivial and narrow,
Not as the great plough tears the tolerant land,
—An acre while you dig your hundred-yard.
Yes, you may hear, across your tidy hedge
A more majestic tillage, quickly-scarred
Arable, turned by coulter ridge on ridge,
Either by heavy horses or by strong
Tractor with driver on the saddle jarred,
Looking across his shoulder at the long
Wake of the furrow, ever on his guard
To swerve no crooked slip;
So as a straightly-navigated ship
Cutting a paler wake with wedge of prow
Leaves port and makes her landfall and her berth
Against a harbour half-across the Earth,
—Miraculous aiming,—goes the steady plough
From heading down to heading, while you stand
Poor gardener, resting on your spade; your hand
Stretching its fingers as a prisoned bird
Flaps wings upon release, by freedom stirred.

Envious you may watch; and after dark
When lassitude has counselled you to bed
The day's work done, (as much as any man
Can do with his small tools and his small strength,
Yet, with all effort, what a little span!)
Then you may hear while winter foxes bark

The sound of tractor travelling the length
Steadily up and down, with beam of light
Straight-streaming as a furrow down the night,
Alive with mist-motes, such a stream, a beam
Hitting the opposite hedgerow with a gleam
As sudden as a shot when startled hare
Leaps from the stubble . . . But the brightest light
Is silent; and you, gardener, can hear
Only the travelling patient sound, so near
Your garden, (as a lover might reprove
For laxity and laggardness in love,)
Since field and garden, plough and spade, must share,
Different in degree but same in character.

Dead season, when you only can prepare
Doggedly for the future, with no hint
Of bright reward, save in your spirit faint
That still believes prophetic in return
Where the Spring sparkles and the Summers burn;
Quittance of labour, rich in recompense,
Your dividend on capital expense,
The interest you had the right to earn
With golden pounds in place of copper pence
Wrested from Winter's brown by Summer's gold.

Dead season, when you knew the world was old
And you yourself far older, and more cold;
A long, unlit, and lamentable plaint.

Then may you turn for comfort to the wall
Where hangs the Dutchman's canvas, mad and bold,
Fervid with fantasy, insensate brawl
Of all your hopes together bunched in paint:

Darkest December, when the flowers fail
And empty tables lack their lucent lading,
And far beyond the window's rainy veil
The landscape stretches into twilight fading
And all seems misted, moribund and pale,
The past too far away for recollection,

The present vacuous, forlorn and stale,
The future far for hope of resurrection,
—Look, then, upon this feast, your eyes regale
On this impossible tumble tossed together,
This freak of Flora's fancy, this all-hail
Regardless of the calendar or weather.
Here is the daffodil, the iris frail,
The peony as blowsy as a strumpet,
The fringèd pink, a summer's draggle-tail,
The gentian funnelled as a tiny trumpet.
Here is the hundred-petalled rose, the hale
Straight streakèd tulip curving like a chalice,
The lily gallant as a ship in sail,
The sinister fritillary of malice,
With pretty nest of thrush or nightingale,
Peaches and grapes cast careless in profusion
That ev'n in paint their warmèd scent exhale
And ripen the extravagant illusion,
All towzled in a crazy fairy-tale
That never blew together in one season
Save where romances over sense prevail,
Yet even here behold the hint of treason:
The small, the exquisite, the brindled snail
Creeping with horny threat towards the foison,
Leaving a glistening, an opal trail,
A smear of evil, signature of poison. . . .

Yet think not you must be of hope bereft
Even when our steep North has rolled
From the life-giving, colour-giving sun
In interval of darkness and of cold,
In loitering length of northern latitude.

Still may you with your frozen fingers cut
Treasures of Winter, if you planted well;
The Winter-sweet against a sheltering wall,
Waxen, Chinese, and drooping bell;
Strange in its colour, almond in its smell;
And the Witch-hazel, *Hamamelis mollis,*
That comes before its leaf on naked bough,

Torn ribbons frayed, of yellow and maroon,
And sharp of scent in frosty English air.

(Why should they be so scented when no insect,
No amorous bee, no evening flitter-moth
Seeks their alluring? Strange, this useless scent!
Shall it charm man alone? an Englishman
Remote from China and her different climate?)

Gardener, if you listen, listen well:
Plant for your winter pleasure, when the months
Dishearten; plant to find a fragile note
Touched from the brittle violin of frost.
Viburnum fragrans, patient in neglect,
That Farrer sent from China;
Patient, and quiet, till, the moment come
When rime all hoar through mist beneath the sun
Turns twigs to little antlers and the grass
To Cinderella's slipper made of glass,—
She breaks, that pale, that fragrant Guelder-rose
As a Court beauty lit at a Court-ball
Sparkled with chandeliers, in muslin youth
Filmy and delicate, yet old as China,
Mobled in roseate surprise
That in December hints at apple-blossom.

She shares that paradox of quality
Of blooms that dare the harsh extremity
Of Winter,—a defiance, it may seem,
Challenge of a fragility extreme
In answer to the fiercest enemy.
Consider: all these winter blooms that grace
Astonishing our dismal winter air,
Are delicate as spirits that oppose
Cynical argument with faith more rare
But not, thereby, less true.
Consider the Algerian iris, frail
As tissue-paper stained in lilac-blue,
Sprung at the foot of wall; consider too
Crocus Tomasianus, small, so pale,

Lavender cups of tiny crockery;
The winter aconite with mint of gold
Like new-struck coins that shame the spectral sun
Hung in our jaundiced heaven,—these are frail,
So frail it seems they scarcely could endure
One touch of horrid life and life's fierce wind.

But Winter holds a gem within its folds,
The brightest diamond in the darkest mine,
Christmas! Yet some will say it also holds
Another jewel in the shortest day.
Oh then we look for lengthening; we look
(Knowing full well that mornings are as dark,)
For that blest moment when, surprised, we say
"It still is light!" and take our torchless way.
Was it the Feast of the Unconquered Sun,
The Roman feast, that fixed the birth of Christ?
The winter solstice welded into one
With the soul's solstice, when we stand and stare
As the sun pauses to regain his height?
This would be suitable: the darkest hour
Slowly revolving to the growing light
As that strange lovely legend entered first
On one small province of expectant world.
Messiah! . . . With the sun He kept a tryst.
The very sun, that ruler of our joy,
Obeyed the mystic birthday, and in power
Grew with the limbs of Mary's little boy.

These may be fancies; none can know or tell
Why in December rings the village bell;
None knows when Christ was born, or sacrificed,
Nor by what Easter was emparadised.
Small matter, at what time the thought of love
Came timeless here to dwell.

It was right, it was suitable,
That all should be
Of the utmost simplicity.

Stable and star . . .
These deeply are
The things we know.
The raftered barn and the usual sky;
England or Palestine, both the same
But for the name;
And the child's first cry.

Jesus a baby; the gentle cow
Looking on, ready to give
Her milk if the Virgin's milk should fail.
As then, as now.
Ready to give, that Messiah should live,
Milk for St. Joseph to squirt in the pail.

Truths surrounding Him at His birth
When He first drew breath;
Such plain and pastoral truths of the barn and the earth.
They stood for the cycle of life, though His end was death,
As the end of us all is death.

And their nostrils gently blew,
Smoking on winter air;
—Nostrils of velvet, udders of silk.
Looking over the wall
That divided stall from stall,
They blew soft scent of pasture and herbs and milk
At the child, as at one of their calves.
No incense, or myrrh.

Great St. Peter and great St. Paul
Travelled far from the stable stall.
Cathedrals, cardinals, all the state,
All the dogma and all the weight,
All the structure of Church and creed,
When Christ in His greater simplicity
Had already given us all we need.

It was right, it was suitable,
That all should be
Of the utmost simplicity
At that Nativity.

And yet, and yet . . . are we not insular,
Relating the familiar to the strange?

I think that Christ was laid in a stone manger,
Not in a manger of warm wood.
It is our English thought that builds of wood
That cosier cot in Palestinian stable;
Our English thought that turns a warm brown barn
Such as we know, into that nursery.

I saw those stone, severe, and Roman mangers
In Timgad, where the Roman horses ate;
And suddenly perceived the likely fact.

Perhaps a little scatter of old straw
Softened that dour, that first prophetic bed;
But stone was His beginning, stone His end.

Pattern of life: the cradle scooped in stone,
That slab of stone at life's end, lying heavy.
Not heavy enough, oh men, oh Roman sentries!
Volatile spirit shifts your lid of stone.

The cradle and the tomb; and in between them
Anguish, and strife, and faith beyond despair.
A resurrection . . . then the pattern wheels
Full cycle back, to find a final limit:
A tomb within the stonier hearts of men.

It snows. How large and soft and slow
The floating flakes that hover down
To find a world of green and brown
And turn it to a world of snow.

In slothful squadrons they alight
That seem to loiter on the way
But still resistless steal the day
And change it to a blaze of white

And blind the night, and with the dawn
Surprise the looker with the change

That turned his world to something strange
The while he slept with curtains drawn.

And still they fall, and still they fall,
A curtain drawn across the skies,
A curtain blinding to the eyes,
That shrouds and shawls a world in pall.

And still they fall, the drifting flakes,
As they would never cease in flight
Inexorably soft and slight
Vanquishing all but streams and lakes,

Until the moment comes when those
Are levelled to a frozen plain
That checks the water's moving vein
And only snow reflects the rose

Of sunrise when no man is by
To see the flush, or at the brink
The thwarted sheep come down to drink,
The disappointed heron fly.

Now for your pleasure and their humble need,
—A double benefit, since you, proud man,
Enjoy the flattery of giving dole
And they, who neither proud nor beggars meek
Will unoffended with imperious beak
Tap in reminder on your window pane
When you, forgetful, richly break your fast
In genial room where hearth and lamplight cast
Their glow on walls though outer world be bleak,—
Set up a table on a solid pole
Outside your window for the ruffled birds.

You may watch them, they you, and who shall say
What thoughts may pass between the minds of each?

But you're superior: you fill a bowl
In careless largess, you the millionaire,
Your pence of crumbs their gold of very life.
Morsels of wealth for morsels of the air.

Yet think not, as you think yourself a lord
Dispensing vail from easy charity,
That you must go without your earned reward.
They, honest debtors, will acquit their score
And you shall not be left the creditor.
Think on the song they gave you, and will give
When the fawn-breasted chaffinch sits once more
On twig-tip perilously perched and singing
Spenser's Epithalamion, and ringing
All bells that ever rang round Easter. . . . Give,
As they will give, who only ask to live.

Meanwhile in many dreary months before
That piercing, pure, ineffable sweet note
Startles you on a morning when your need
For resurrection is most urgent, then
When spring calls loud, and sap begins to rise
Up through the trunks of trees and trunks of men,—
Throughout the silent months the silent birds
May bring a pleasure to your watching eyes,
A private, simple pleasure, not for words.
Observe, how dangling blue-tits peck the seed
You saved from stalks of plaintain; and the wren
Small as a mouse and browner than a mouse,
Too light to bend a reed,
Snatches a darting battle in her greed
That is no greed, but hunger, when the cold
Such timorous and anxious mites makes bold.

You watcher at the window, you who know
Life's danger, and how narrow is the line,
How slight the structure of your happiness,
—Think on these little creatures in the snow.
They are so fragile and so fine,
So pitiably small, so lightly made,
So brave and yet so very much afraid.
They die so readily, with all their song.

Yet think not they are friendly or secure
As you with your intentions kind and pure;

119

Your echoes of Saint Francis down the long
Humane tradition from Assisi borne
In charitable thought of human mind.
Oh no! they're quarrelsome because forlorn;
They fight for life; and, frightened, flit away
Even from your good table, snatching crumbs
To eat within the hedge, however kind
Your meaning be, set up on pole or spike.
It is not you they fear, but one another.
—Christ would have said that bird to bird was brother,
But Christ and Nature seldom speak alike.

It thaws. The hand of Winter slackens grip.
"Wind's changed," he said, the old the lonely man
Out in the woods at work before the dawn.
"Wind's changed." It seemed as summoning a phrase
As a thanksgiving to an answered prayer.
I looked, and saw above the hill-top pines
Reddened by sunrise, that the whitened vanes
Had swung. "The wind's gone round," he surly said,
Stooping to adze his frosty chestnut spiles.

It thaws. The fingers of the Winter drip.
They weaken into water, as a heart
Melted by love. They are no longer cruel.
They change their mind, as wind has changed its mind.
They let the tiles upon the roofs appear,
Brown in their ordinary character;
They let the hedges in their lines appear
Black in their winter custom; let the grass
Show through the snow for hungry sheep to find.
It thaws, and through the night that was so still
When the moon rose above the fields of snow
Now comes the sound of water pouring down
Over the sluice within the dip of valley.
Something of beauty goes. This clean clean world
So strangely silent of unwalken snow
Printed by bird-claw and the pad of fox,
Turns to a dirty thing, a compromise,
Patchy and smudged, and all too like our life.

Yet will the anxious peering gardener go,
Looking for broken branches, buckled paths.
He knows that underground his plants are safe
Since snow is warm not cold; and thinks with relish
Of little Alpines in accustomed cot
With their white rug, a northern Silver Fleece,
Not Golden as the ram that flew from Greece.

He knows them safe; but still he greatly fears
Fresh frost to follow on the kindly thaw,
When the dread ice-rain, chain-mail, clattering,
Clothes in a curtain all his tender sprigs—
(Cruelty after kindness comes more harsh
As kindness after cruelty more sweet.)
Also, if he be wise, as gardeners are,
He'll knock the melting snow as hedges bend
Under wet weight, and curtsey to the ground
Flexible wands of yew and edging-box.

And then with thaw comes up the sudden rush

Of growth that waited only on this hour,
On this disclosure of the life beneath.
As the slow secret movement in the life
Of men and nations in their multitude
Blanketed by oppression, poverty,
And lack of light,—oh mostly lack of light—
So on a sudden with the genial sun
The aspiration of the myriad crowd
Of pushing leaves and buds within their sheath
Leaps with new motive in a long prepared
Attack to pierce the slowly softening earth.
A gentle mutiny; a pretty change;
Haste without violence; and then a flower
More lovely than mankind has ever brought to birth.

Here leap the leaves, where none before were seen;
Swords of narcissus and of daffodil,
A sheaf of blades, too flexible, too green
(It seems) to thrust their points; yet they appear
From nowhere in a night and with the morn are here.
Likewise the iris, that had sunk to ground
In sodden mass of infelicity
Lifts up her grass-green spear,
And these are signs of spring, that spurious spring
That comes in February to astound
And, against reason, make our hearts believe.

The yellow crocus through the grass will bring
Her light as pointed as a candle flame,
Not there at sunrise, but at midday there.
And snowdrops that increase each year,
Each leaf so tipped with white
As though it too desired to bear a flower.

Now in odd corners you may find
Enough for little bunches, as a child
Will bring you in hot hand a drooping gift
Dragged from the hedges and the cranny wild,
The daisy and the campion and the thrift,

Too dead to save, but if your heart be kind
Too dear to throw away
Until the giver on some other quest
Darts off to find a blackbird on her nest
Or, dropped along the road, a wisp of hay.

But these your winter bunches, jealously
Picked on a February morning, they
Are dearer than the plenteous summer. See,
One coloured primrose growing from a clump,
One Lenten rose, one golden aconite,
Dog Toby in his ruff, with varnish bright,
One sprig of daphne, roseate or white,
One violet beneath a mossy stump,
One gold and purple iris, brave but small
Child of the Caucasus, and bind them all
Into a tussie-mussie packed and tight
And envy not the orchid's rich delight.

Shall I count March in Winter? yes, in this
Dear northern island where the sun's late kiss
Comes not till middle April. We believe
Too readily in pledges that deceive.
In one day's promise of a warming air,
In one day's painting by a stronger sun
That on a sudden with a flying flare
Deepens the shadows underneath the arch
And touches all the tips to buds where none
Yesterday showed, and sweeps a generous brush
Across plantations of the ignoble larch,
Across the lovelier copse
With undefinable but certain flush
Lingering on the catkins and the tops
Of hazel and the sticky chestnut, when
The small brown things are blown across the ground
Between the fallen twigs and stubs and stones,
—A leaf, a mouse, a wren?—
All in a hurry in the wind of March.

Then in the garden where the skeleton

Leaves of the hornbeam rattle their brown bones
Soon to be pushed aside
As pitiless youth comes on
Shoving and rowdy, crying out "Make way!"
Young savages that mean to have their day,
Those little waves of an audacious tide
That, yesterday unnoted and unseen,
Turned in one night senility's decay
To the fresh life of inexperienced green,
—Then, gardener, though you be an agèd man
And soon to lie where lie the twisted roots,
Seize on your last advantage while you can;
Sing your last lyric with the sappy shoots.

Sow from your packets on the finely-raked
Patches in autumn sweetened with the slaked
Lime that corrects an acid soil
And crumbles obstinate clay
To lessen your stiff toil;
(As the wood-ashes from your open hearth
Piling too high and gray
Will softly lighten and with potash feed
The clamant earth,
From fire's destruction to creation's need
Aptly returned.) Sow broad and liberal,
But thinly spaced, for plants no less than men
Ask space to be themselves, no sunless den
Where lank and dank they narrow to a weed.
Be generous and nature will repay.
See how one seedling, fallen all by chance
In some forgotten corner, as a stray,
Spreads sturdy as a little bush and takes
A yard of space, no cramping to an inch,
And in its freedom breaks
Into fresh growth without your vigilance
That comes to stop and pinch
And train and foster in the straitened way.

This lesson learn from Nature, and observe.
So might some waif of genius, strangely sprung,

Flower in our English tongue,
Divinely foolish and divinely young;
Some poet from a scrap-heap, some new Keats
Full of wild images and rich conceits,
Breaking untrammelled, from convention free,
Speak the large language that we still deserve.

But you, oh gardener, poet that you be
Though unaware, now use your seeds like words
And make them lilt with colour nicely flung
Where colour's wanted, light as humming-birds;
For these your annuals are light of heart,
Delicate in their texture, brief of life,
Making the most of their impetuous part;
Sweet irresponsibles of youth, or death;
No middle-age; they nothing know between:
No solemn roots for them who riot rife,
Flipping their progeny to fates unseen
Wind-borne or bird-borne, fugitive as breath,
Springing where they have fallen in a new
Quick fanfare of existence gaily spent,
None knowing whence they came or where they went,
Only that they were freshened with the dew
And died with frost when Nature proved unkind,
For they had only beauty; only knew
Life in a happy summer; had no mind
For schemes protective when the troubles came,
But died, and left a label with their name.

Their names were nymphs, and they were nymphs indeed,
A whole mythology from pinch of seed.
Nemesia and Viscaria, and that
Blue-as-the-butterfly Phacelia;
Love-in-mist Nigella, whose strong brat
Appears unwanted like a very weed;
Nemōphila,—I knew a little boy
Who called his doll Nemōphila, for joy
In that Greek word he fitted to a toy;
But there's no end within a list that sheds
Petals on summer, seeds on autumn beds,

A list elaborate as chime of bells
Known to the ringer in their composite peal
Where difficult art must difficult skill conceal,
Each separately used but woven in their time
To make the melody of perfect chime
Over the listening landscape richly rolled;
So does the gardener choose a list to hold
Sweet Sultan and Sweet Alyssum that smells
Of sea-cliffs and short turf
Where move the cropping sheep
And sea-gulls waver sprinkled round the steep
Crags that descend into the constant surf;
A list of mignonette and marigold
And other pretty things,
But lest you be romancefully inclined
Thinking that beauty unattended springs
All jilly-jolly from your scatterings,
Let dull instruction here remind
That mignonette is tricky, and demands
Firm soil, and lime, to follow your commands,
Else failure comes, and shows a barren space
Where you had looked for small but scented spires.

Yet you more easily may light the fires
Of Summer with the Californian
Poppy, and the Siberian
Wallflower, twanging both their orange lyres
Even too loudly with a lack of grace,
Vulgar but useful (as we mostly are,)
Splashing more sunlight on a sunny place,
A rug of such shrill colour, seen afar
Down the long vista, cast in gold surprise
At foot of yellow lupins that arise
As full of honey as the laden bees
Powdered with pollen on their Ethiop thighs.

Malapert March is parent to all these,
The sowing-time, when warmth begins to creep
Into the soil, as he who handles earth

With his bare hand well knows, and, stooping, feels
The sun on his bare nape, and as he kneels
On pad of sacking knows the stir of birth
Even as woman quickened stirs from sleep
And knows before all others in the deep
Instinct's communion that so much reveals,
The rite of the immediate future; so
Does the good gardener sense propitious time
And sows when seeds may grow
In the warm soil that follows on the rime
And on the breaking frost and on the snow.

And then in safety shall he prune
The rose with slicing knife above the bud
Slanting and clean; and soon
See the small vigour of the canted shoots
Strike outwards in their search for light and air,
Lifted above the dung about their roots,
Lifted above the mud.
Yet, unlike fashion's votary, beware
Of pruning so that but the stumps remain,
Miserly inches for the little gain
Of larger flower, exhibition's boast.
Neglect may hold a beauty of her own;
Neglected gardens in these years of war
When the fond owner wandered as a ghost
Only in thought, and longed to cut and trim
Having a vision of his roses prim
As they should be, what time the month was flown,
—Such gardens and their roses over-grown
As never in their careful life before
Flung to the daylight and the scented dark
With no man there to mark
A free and splendid tossing in a host
As unexpected as it had been rare.

But winter passes. March is not yet done
Before the solace of a warmer sun
Strokes on our hands and takes us by surprise

With a forgotten touch on naked skin.
The almond breaks to pink against the skies;
Then do we start, and with new-opened eyes
See the true Spring begin.
It flowers in the grass beneath our feet
Where yesterday the colour sparse and thin
Of some rathe daffodil blew here, or there,
Not more than two or three,
Like slender tinkle of a clavecin
In a light sprinkle, single, stray, and rare,
That overnight has flowed into a fleet
Of yellow sails to ride the grassy sea.

Then in a hurry where they all compete
Spearing upon each other's tracks in haste
To catch their chance of life, by sun set free,
—Oh, what intoxication of the air!—
Come crowding all the chaste
And adolescent children of the Spring.
Their music rises like the violin
Taking her place in a full symphony,
Piercing unbearably, so tart, so sweet,
As flying notes upon the air take wing
To twang within our heart an answered string.
Then all the earth is bright with clean and neat
Stars of the Apennine anemone,
And coloured primrose cousin of the mild
Insipid primrose in the wood's retreat,
And varnished celandine, that golden child
Unwanted of prolific March; then fling
The sterile cherries in a canopy
Translucent branches over and among
The pavement of the flowers, in a wild
Storm of successive blossom, lightly swung,
So lightly it would seem that they took wing
Also, in notes ethereal, and with Spring
Taught us again the sense of being young.

So March tips over, as a watershed
Where runnels southward send their little race

Towards a greener land, and grow and spread
Till all the fertile veins of water lace
The slopes towards the waiting valley, fed
By snows of Winter, in a hurrying chase
To reach the dry and bony river-bed
And green its banks that like a skeleton
Seemed finally and desperately dead.

SPRING

"APRIL is the cruellest month, breeding
Lilacs out of the dead land, mixing
Memory and desire, stirring
Dull roots with spring rain."

Would that my pen like a blue bayonet
Might skewer all such cats'-meat of defeat;
No buttoned foil, but killing blade in hand.
The land and not the waste land celebrate,
The rich and hopeful land, the solvent land,
Not some poor desert strewn with nibbled bones,
A land of death, sterility, and stones.

We know that the ultimate vex is the same for all:
The discrepancy
Between the vision and the reality.
When this has been said, the last sad word is said.
There is nothing to add but the fact that we had the vision,
And this was a grace in itself, the decision
We took between hope and despond;

The different way that we heard and accepted the call;
The different way
We tried to respond.

Let me respond my way, construct my theme
From particles of a different dream,
Be it illusion as well it may.
I would sooner hope and believe
Than dig for my living life a present grave.
Though I must die, the only thing I know,
My only certainty, so far ahead
Or just around the corner as I go,
Not knowing what the dangerous turn will bring,
Only that some one day I must be dead,
—I still will sing with credence and with passion
In a new fashion
That I will believe in April while I live.
I will believe in Spring,
That custom of the year, so frail, so brave,
Custom without a loss of mystery.

April the angel of the months, the young
Love of the year. Ancient and still so young,
Lovelier than the craven's paradox;
Christ's Easter and the Syrian Adonis'
When all things turn into their contrary,
Death into life and silence into sound;
When all the bells of Rome
Leap from their Lenten lull, and all the birds,
—Small bells more myriad than the Roman bells;
And all the flow'rs like Botticelli's flow'rs
Small, brilliant, close to earth, and youngly gay.

The Pasque-flow'r which ignores
A date the moon ordained, but takes its rule
From sun and rain, as both by chance occur;
Yet some years by a nice coincidence
Opens upon our very Easter-day
(When the sun dances or is said to dance,)
Lavender petals sheathed in silver floss

SPRING

Soft as the suffle of a kitten's fur;
That pulsatilla, 'shaken by the wind',
That fragile native of the chalky Downs;

Innumerable, the small flow'rs that stitch
Their needlework on canvas of the ground.
In the low foreground of their tapestry
They startle and exceedingly enrich.
There's a profusion hardly to be counted
When flow'r from bulb appears with each new Spring,
Like to a spring of water newly founted,
Breaking the earth, and each an Easterling.

Bubbles of colour striking through the bleak
Dun soil, surprising, in a week,
As the low desert-flowers after rain
Leap into being where they were not seen
Few hours before, and soon are gone again.
So in our English garden comes the Greek
Blue wind-flow'r, cousin of the meek
Bashful anemone of English woods,
As thick as shingle strewn on Chesil Beach;
So comes the Lady Tulip, with her streak
Of pink that ribs her white; and through the green
Of young fine grass, the Glory of the Snow,
So blue, a smear of fallen sky; come each
In quick succession as they grow and blow
In liberal April, host to little guests:

The azure scilla, and the indigo
Grape-hyacinth in cluster like the breasts
Of the Ephesian mother of the earth,
Fecund Diana, and from seed self-sown
Running between the cracks of paving-stone
In rivulets of blue will wind and flow.
So lavish all, so piercing, and so bright
That all the words of all the tongues of men are worth
Not one quick instant's sight.

Yet, sealed upon the wax of memory,

Certain imprints, as in a peepshow's frame,
Brilliant and artificial, catch the light
To burn forever with a coloured flame
Always within the mind, chameleon,
Flaring the saddened corners and the doom.
The place, the hour, the flow'r, may have no name;
Is it Mycenae or the Lebanon?
Mycenae where the wild-flow'r rugs are spread
For the wild bees that hive in Agamemnon's tomb
Though Helen's false and Menelaus dead?
Is it the Lebanon that looks across
To Palestine and throws the cedar shade
To touch the greater shadow of the Cross
Though Christ be slain and Mary still a Maid?
It matters not, it matters not a shred
Whence beauty comes, if beauty only be
Held in the heart with love her constant twin,
Great myths that answer many a mystery.

The Syrian ranges and the Grecian mound. . . .
Or simpler painting of our English ground
As varied as the cloak of harlequin.
See, down the nut-plat, washing in a tide
That laves each inch of soil, the manifold
Wealth of the coloured primrose, thick and wide,
Butter-and-eggs, with stripes of tiger-skin,
And saffron lakes, all shot with sun, and pied,
And clumps of polyanthus laced with gold.

The leopard's camouflage, the lion's pride,
Were not more freckled, tawny, than this mob
Matted in clusters, lowly, and so dense
They hide the earth beneath their opulence;
And down the colonnades of Kentish cob
Two little statues, one at either end,
Wistfully watch each other through the years,
Parted for ever, that can only send
Messages from their eyes too hard for tears;
Eros and Aphrodite, in defeat,
The prince of love, the queen of loveliness,
Never to touch and never to caress
Since from their pedestals they cannot move to meet.

Weave the poor poet all his ablest words
Into a poacher's snare, a springle set,
Making a mesh of pretty nouns his string
With knots of adjective and epithet,
Simple, felicitous, or richly grand,
—The finch of beauty struggles through the net
And bearing off her gold upon the wing
Is gone, uncaught, into a different air,
He knows not where,
Only that she is not within his hand.

Such days, such days so wealthy and so warm
As tempt the very busy bees to swarm,
Make the articulate poet silent; live
Instead of speaking; leave his desk and leave
His books, his foolscap, and the blue-black ink
Drying upon his pen as the sun falls
Hot on his table, beating on the walls.

How blessèd to exist and not to think!

He becomes one with Nature, sensitive
Only to that which happens, as the bee;
He is both permanent and fugitive;
He is the mole, the weasel, or the hawk;

He is the seed, the first leaf, and the stalk;
He grows, he breathes, he lives, and he is free,
Child of the sun and of the stroking air
Warming as he emerges from his door
As though he pushed aside
The leathern curtain of cathedral porch
In Italy, and came outside
Followed by incense, to the pavement's scorch,
And shrank from glare of marble to the shade
Rounded in caverns of the curved arcade.

But in this dear delusion of a South
Which never was and never can be ours,
Drowsy, voluptuous, and rich in sloth,
We northerners must turn towards our flowers.
They are our colour; brave, they are our flags;
A living substitute for marble swags;
They flutter as the dressing of a ship,
Long pennants that in breezes blow and dip,
Gay as the washing of Venetian rags,
Cracking in colour as the lash of whip
Fine in the air, or as a feathered phrase,
An arrow shot of poetry or prose,
And each a note within a hymn of praise.
April's the busy month, the month that grows
Faster than hand can follow at its task;
No time to relish and no time to bask,
(Though when indeed is that the gardener's lot,
However large, however small his plot?)
April's the month for pruning of the rose,
April's the month when the good gardener sows
More annuals for summer, cheap and quick,
Yet always sows too thick
From penny packets scattered on a patch
With here a batch of poppy, there a batch
Of the low candytuft or scabious tall
That country children call
Pincushions, with their gift
Of accurate observance and their swift
Naming more vivid than the botanist.

So the good gardener will sow his drift
Of larkspur and forget-me-not
To fill blank space, or recklessly to pick;
And gay nasturtium writhing up a fence
Splotching with mock of sunlight sunless days
When latening summer brings the usual mist.

He is a millionaire for a few pence.
Squandering Nature in her gift exceeds
Even her own demands.
Consider not the lily, but her seeds
In membrane tissue packed within the pod
With skill that fools the skill of human hands;
The poppy with her cracking pepper-pot
That spills in ripened moment split asunder;
The foxglove with her shower fine as snuff.
Consider these with thankfulness and wonder,
Nor ever ask why that same God
If it was He who made the flow'rs, made weeds:

The thistle and the groundsel with their fluff;
The little cresses that in waste explode
Mistaken bounty at the slightest touch;
The couch-grass throwing roots at every node,
With wicked nick-names like its wicked self,
Twitch, quitch, quack, scutch;
The gothic teazle, tall as hollyhock,
Heraldic as a halberd and as tough;
The romping bindweed and the rooting dock;
The sheeny celandine that Wordsworth praised,
(He was no gardener, his eyes were raised;)
The dandelion, cheerful children's clock
Making a joke of minutes and of hours,
Ironical to us who wryly watch;
Oh why, we ask, reversing good intentions,
Was Nature so ingenious in inventions,
And why did He who must make weeds, make flowers?

Let us forget the sorrows: they are there

Always, but Spring too seldom there;
Once in a life-time only; oh seize hold!
Sweet in the telling once, but not re-told.
In Nature's cycle blessèd once a year,
Not long enough to savour, but more dear
For all the anguish of its brevity.

Then in the poignant moment made aware
We are all things, the flower and the tree,
Detail of petal, and the general burst
Greening the valley and th' horizon hurst;
The bud still folded and the bud fulfilled;
We are the distant landscape and the near.
We are the drought, we are the dew distilled;
The saturated land, the land athirst;
We are the day, the night, the light, the dark;
The water-drop, the stream; the meadow and the lark.

We are the picture, and the hand that paints;
The trodden pathway, and the foot that trod;
We are the humble echo of great saints
Who knew that God was all, and all was God.

Look round for truth when truth is near at hand,
So simple now it seems but life and love,
—Perhaps the general answer to a scheme
So strangely ciphered that in our extreme
Perplexity we stand
Most piteously duped by foolish feints.

Small is our vision, rare the searchlight beam;
Few moments given but in truth supreme.
Transcendent moments, when the simpler theme
Is suddenly perceived
And by our intricate uncertainty
We are no more deceived.

Resurgent May, softness with energy,

Warmth after cold, reunion after loss.
It is a columbarium full of doves,
A susurration of the living leaves.
Murmur, old music; Sun, shake out your locks,
That heavy fleece, that rowelled aureole;
But in th' intoxication of this spilth
Let us be stolid as the flood arrives;
Practise a difficult sobriety,
Keep hold on wits, not lose them in the fierce
Draughts of such wine. Not think on spurious heaven,
—The drunkard's heaven in a bottle sealed,
The lover's heaven in a woman's arms,
The miser's heaven in a bag of coins,
Or this the poet's and the gardener's heaven
When all comes true, collusive flattery
Of consummation waiting on desire.

Not think on heaven, for we tread on earth
And must stay soberly about our business,
Anchored to realism, knowing well
That there's no pausing for complacency
But only vision of a better future;
Next year, not this year, therefore must we turn
Our glance from present pleasure, and prepare.
Always prepare: the urge, the wish to travel
Forward, and never rest on point of time.

Therefore the while your current wall-flow'rs blow,
—Bronze as a pheasant, ruby as old wine
Held up against the light,—in string-straight line
Next year's supply on seed-bed you shall sow
Unless an early drought postpone till June,
And watch the little seedlings as they grow,
Thinning them out, for far too generous
The generative warmth of amorous bed;
(Friable fistfuls of the soil are warm
To naked hand) and a kind discipline
Shall later check the young impetuous growth,
Stopping the very centre of their impulse,

Incomprehensibly, with cruel-kind
Slice of the knife aslant through sappy shoot,
And from that wound shall sturdier bushes spring.

And thus shall all biennials have your care,
Sown in their drills in May, that the full year
May pass before their last accomplishment;
The bell-flow'rs, and the Indian pinks; Sweet Rocket,
Scabious and hollyhock and Honesty.

But also think on more immediate months
And bring those annuals that fear the frost,
Loving the sun, more splendid for their briefness,
Out from their boxes sheltered under glass:
Mexican zinnias and the Texan phlox,
African marigolds, all bright exotics;
And sow when danger of the frost is past
Generous sprinklings of night-scented stock,
Dingy and insignificant and plain,
But speaking with a quiet voice at dusk.

These for the Summer; and with heedful eye
Quick as a hatching bird, the gardener roves
Precautionary, nipping mischief's bud.
For mischief buds at every joint and node,
Plentiful as the burgeon of the leaves:
Fungus and mildew, blight and spot and rust,
Canker and mould, a sallow sickly list;
The caterpillar that with hump and heave
Measures the little inches of his way;
And, pullulating more than Tartar hordes,
Despoiling as they travel, procreation
Calamitous in ravage, multitude
Unnumbered, come the insect enemies,
Tiny in sevralty, in union dire,
Clustered as dense as pile in plush—the aphis
Greening the hopeful shoot, the evil ant
Armoured like daimios, in horrid swarm
Blackening twigs, or hidden down their hole

Mining amongst the roots till flagging heads
Of plants betray their presence.
                                        Gardener,
Where is your armistice? You hope for none.
It will not be, until yourself breed maggots.

Moles from the meadow will invade your plot;
Pink palm, strong snout, and velvet energy
Tunnel a system worthy of a sapper;
Heave monticules while you lie snug-a-bed,
And heave again, fresh chocolate, moist mould,
In mounds that show their diligent direction,
Busy while you but break your nightly fast,
Visible evidence of secret work,
And overground the nimble hopping rabbit
Soft as a baby's toy, finds out the new
Cosseted little plants with tender hand
Set out in innocence to do their duty.
Poor gardener! poor stubborn simpleton,
Others must eat, though you be bent on beauty.
Yet you have allies in this freakish scheme
Of nature's contradictions. The good bee,
Unconscious agent; and the funny hedgehog;
The toad you nearly step on, blebbed and squat;
The glow-worm, little torch that bores its light
Into the shelly cavern of the snail;
The lady-bird, the Bishop Barnaby,
So neat in oval spotted carapace,
A joke to children, but to aphides
A solemn foe. . . . Oh curious little world,
Nether, yet paralleled against our own.

And more demands exact the gardener's care.
Those reckless buds, those ill-advisèd shoots!
"A tie so soon prevents their doom" they say,
So stake before the havoc of the gale,
The rough South-west that wears a cloak of rain,
But whether bruzzy hazel-tops you choose
Or pointed sticks from handy spinney cut,

Or bought bamboo,—set early into place
That growing plants may hide the artifice
And of your cunning cover up the trace.

Then for a moment may you pause, an hour
To let the snake of satisfaction creep,
Writhing round corners, slithering down paths,
Rustling through grass, and, like that other serpent
Whispering in that other garden, tempt
To snug complacency, that foe to wisdom.
"Here you succeeded; this you plotted well;
Here did you turn the stream of Nature's will,
Damming the wilderness of her invasion;
Here did you triumph, here did you compel;
Here took advantage of a happy hazard;
Here, like a poet, made your colours rhyme;
Here, like a painter, made your pattern plain.
Rest now; enjoy; sit back; the years slip on
With many a little death before the last
Orgulous swordsman like a matador
Thrusts, and has done. The many little deaths,
Death of the ear, the half-death of the eye,
The muscle limping where it ran, the loss
Of strength that gradual as a dropping wind
Becalms the still-spread sails. Worst wane of all,
A lessening most hardly to be borne,
The pricking banderillas of the years
Bleed from your flanks in loss of that most precious
Zest of endeavour and anticipation,
Jewels of youth, those undivided twins
That live and die by one another's breath
And have no separate being."

Dangerous counsel ever caught the ear,
Yet for that pleasing moment, not unduly
Prolonged, consider now the fruits of labour:
The tulips, that have pushed a pointed tusk
In steady inches, suddenly resolve
Upon their gesture. Earliest the royal
Princes of Orange and of Austria,

Their courtier the little Duc van Thol,
And, since the State must travel with the Church,
In plum-shot crimson, Couleur Cardinal.
But grander than these dwarfs diminutive,
Comes the tall Darwin with the waxing May.
Can stem so slender bear such sovereign head
Nor stoop with weight of beauty? See, her pride
Equals her beauty; never grew so straight
A spire of faith, nor flew so bright a flag
Lacquered by brush-stroke of the painting sun.
And in the darkest corner of a room
One sheaf of tulips splashes; it illumes,
Challenge to mournfulness, so clean, so kempt,
As in the garden, brilliant regiment,
Their stretch illumes the distance.
                                   In their range
From the white chastity of Avalanche
They pass through yellow of the buttercup
To cherry and the deepening red of blood
Violently based on dark electric blue;
All sheen, all burnish, orient as the pearl;
Lavender fringed with silver; royal purple
Growing more sonorous in glossy black
Of Faust and Sultan and La Tulipe Noire.
Ah, there were floods of tulips once in Holland;
There were old loving men with expert fingers,
Leading the better life of courtesy.

And if to vary the severity
Of single colour in a single flower
Your thoughts incline, set separate a patch
Of broken sports, by purist not esteemed
But loved by painters for the incidence
Of wayward streak and hint of porcelain.

The Rembrandt tulip, leather-brown and white
So finely feathered, brush of sable's hair
Never laid more exact, nor monkish clerk
Dusted his gold-leaf with more spare a hand;

Or the Bizarre in broken rose-and-white,
A china cup, a polished cup up-held
(Too maidenly; I cannot like so well;)
Or else the Parrot, better called the Dragon,
Ah, that's a pranking feat of fantasy,
Swirling as crazy plumes of the macaw,
Green flounced with pink, and fringed, and topple-heavy
A tipsy flower, lurching with the fun
Of its vagary. Has it strayed and fallen
Out of the prodigal urn, the Dutchman's canvas
Crammed to absurdity? or truly grown
From a brown bulb in brown and sober soil?

So cosmopolitan, these English tulips,
To cottager as native as himself!
Aliens, that Shakespeare neither saw nor sang.
Alien Asiatics, that have blown
Between the boulders of a Persian hill
Long centuries before they reached the dykes
To charm van Huysum and the curious Brueghel,
And Rachel Ruysch, so nice so leisurely
That seven years were given to two pictures.

Tulip, *dulband*, a turban; rare
Persian that wanders in our English tongue.

How fair the flowers unaware
That do not know what beauty is!
Fair, without knowing they are fair,
With poets and gazelles they share
Another world than this.

They can but die, and not betray
As friends or love betray the heart.
They can but live their pretty day
And do no worse than simply play
Their brief sufficient part.

They cannot break the heart, as friend
Or love may split our trust for ever.

We never asked them to pretend:
Death is a clean sufficient end
For flower, friend, or lover.

SUMMER

SWEET JUNE. Is she of Summer or of Spring,
Of adolescence or of middle-age?
A girl first marvelling at touch of lovers
Or else a woman growing ripely sage?
Between the two she delicately hovers,
Neither too rakish nor, as yet, mature.
She's not a matron yet, not fully sure;
Neither too sober nor elaborate;
Not come to her fat state.
She has the leap of youth, she has the wild
Surprising outburst of an earnest child.
Sweet June, dear month, while yet delay
Wistful reminders of a dearer May;
June, poised between, and not yet satiate.

What pleasant sounds: the scythe in the wet grass
Where ground's too rough for the machine to pass,
(Grass should be wet for a close cut, the blade
Hissing like geese as swathe by swathe is laid;)

The pigeons on the roof, the hives aswarm;
June is the month of sounds. They melt and merge
Softer than shallow waves in pebbled surge
Forward and backward in a summer cove;
The very music of the month is warm,
The very music sings the song of love.

Such murmurous concert all our sense confounds.
The breath within the trees
Is it of doves or bees,
Or our own ripened heart
That must take part
Adding its cadence to the symphonies
Of June, that month of sounds?

That month of sounds, that month of scents,
That sensuous month when every sense
Ripens, and yet is young;
Th' external world, by which we judge
And sterner rules of reason grudge;
That dear misleading framework of our faith,
Truth in untruth, that picture slung
From such precarious nail; that nectarous breath
Of music, when the senses grow confused
And each might be the other; when, bemused,
We stray through thickets of the honeyed air.
But, Wanderer, then beware
Of beanfields amorous to strolling lovers,
Too dangerous (they say) to dally there
Along the hedgerow by the serried coverts
Where murmuring cushats hint that love is fair.
No sweeter load was ever laid at eve
Across the shoulders of the country's sweep
Mantled in June that, drowsing, seem asleep
But stir to greet the dream that all believe.

June of the iris and the rose.
The rose not English as we fondly think.
Anacreon and Bion sang the rose;
And Rhodes the isle whose very name means rose

Struck roses on her coins;
Pliny made lists and Roman libertines
Made wreaths to wear among the flutes and wines;
The young Crusaders found the Syrian rose
Springing from Saracenic quoins,
And China opened her shut gate
To let her roses through, and Persian shrines
Of poetry and painting gave the rose.

The air of June is velvet with her scent,
The realm of June is splendid with her state.
Asia and Europe to our island lent
These parents of our rose,
Yet Albion took her name from her white rose
Not from her cliffs, some say. So let it be.
We know the dog-rose, flinging free
Whip-lashes in the hedgerow, starred with pale
Shell blossom as a Canterbury Tale,
The candid English genius, fresh and pink
As Chaucer made us think,
Singing of adolescent meads in May.
That's not the rose in her true character;
She's a voluptuary; think of her
Wine-dark and heavy-scented of the South,
Stuck in a cap or dangled from a mouth
As soft as her own petals. That's the rose!
No sentimentalist, no maiden sweet,
Appealing, half-forlorn,
But deep and old and cunning in deceit,
Offering promises too near the thorn.
She is an expert and experienced woman
Wearing her many faces
Pleasing to different men in different places;
She plays the madrigal when moist with dew
To charm the English in their artless few,
But at her wiser older broad remove
Remains an Asiatic and a Roman,
Accomplice of the centuries and love.

Dangerous beauty we have sometimes seen,

Dangerous moments we have sometimes had.
Thus I saw floating in a sunken pool
A pavement of red roses in Baghdad.

A floating floor of dark beheaded blood
Between blue tiles that feigned to look so cool,
And that was beauty, sunk in liquid floor
Of roses and of water red as war,
But other visions took me on their flood
To other blood-red points where I had been:

St. Mark's in Venice on an Easter-day
Deep as the petals of Arabian rose,
When a great Cardinal in robes arose
Tremendous in the pulpit, and began
"Così diceva lo scrittor pagan" . . . .
Virgil a living presence in the church;
Lambent mosaics, tarnished in their gold,
And all things heavy with their age, so old
They seemed as distant as my own lost search.

Those blood-red roses floating in the pool,
That blood-red lamp above the altar slung,
Were they identical, or I a fool?
God's lamp His own red rose, where censers swung?

Heavy July. Too rampant and too lush;
High Summer, dull, fulfilled, and satiate,
Nothing to fear, and little to await.
The very birds are hush.
Dark over-burdened woods: too black, their green.

No leaping promise, no surprise, no keen
Difficult fight against a young, a lean
Sharp air and frozen soil; no contest bright
Of fragile courage winning in despite.
Easy July, when all too warmly blows
The surfeit of the rose
Risking no harm;
And those aggressive indestructible

Bores, the herbaceous plants, that gladly take
Whatever's given and make no demand
Beyond the careless favour of a stake;
Humble appeal, not arrogant command,
Like some tough spinster, doughty, duteous,
All virtue and no charm.

I have no love for such fulfilment, none.
Too sweet, the English rain; too soft, the sun.
Too rank, midsummer in our gently moist
Island that never riots to extremes.
Moderate beauty, yet insidious,
The veils that magicked Shakespeare into dreams;
England, as douce as any woman's muff.

Where is the violence, the shrilly-voiced
Cicada of the arid plain?
Where the intransigence of Afric Spain?
Where are the stones, the fireflies, and the rough
Danger of mountain road?
Skeletons like the ribs of ships
Where beasts have fallen, broken by their load?
Even the aloe, used as cruel goad?
Sunlight on columns, lizards on the rocks?
There is another landscape, and my blood
Nostalgic stirs; I think upon the flocks
Raggedly seeking pasture in the scrub,
But must content myself with hollyhocks
And moisture-loving phlox
And the obliging shrub
Here in my lovely island, tender, safe,
While yet I chafe
For sunburnt wastes the colour of the fox.

Too tame, too smug, I cry;
There's no adventure in security;
Yet still my little garden craft I ply,
Mulch, hoe, and water when the ground is dry;
Cut seeding heads; thin out the stoning fruit;
Cut out th' unwanted, tie the wanted, shoot;

Weed paths that with one summer shower of rain
For all my labour are as green again.
And so strive on, for there is no repose
Even though Summer redden with the rose.
Slug, snail, and aphis force a busy day,
With traps of orange-peel and lettuce-leaves to lay,
And buckets of insecticide to spray.
Black Spot, Red Rust, Red Spider, all the scale
Of enemy controlled by frothy pail,
Soft-soap and quassia chips, a murderous bath,
And in the evening note the hob-nail trail
Of slime, and crush the snail
Brittle as biscuit on the garden path.

(Here will the mottled thrush your helpmate be
With tap tap tap in secret carpentry
As one who hammers on a distant nail,
Heard, but too rarely seen.)

Now will the water-lilies stain the lake
With cups of yellow, chalices of cream,
Set in their saucer leaves of olive-green
On greener water, motionless, opaque,
—This haunt of ducks, of grebes, and poacher herns.
Now is the stillness deeper than a dream;
Small sounds, small movements shake
This quietude, that deeper then returns
After the slipping of the water-snake,
The jump of trout, the sudden cry of coot,
The elegiac hoot
Of owls within the bordering wood, that take
The twilight for their own.
This is their hour, and mine; we are alone;
I drift; I would that I might never wake.

Wake to a world where all important seem
Immediate actions in our little scheme,
Trifles of urgency, our warp and weft.
There is another world that doubles this poor world,
Where intimations like a source, a stream

Sprung from a rock by bolt of vision cleft
Crowd on the spirit in an hour too brief
But in its stab, extreme.

Mine be those hours, their value, and their theft.
Are they the thief, or is the world the thief?
Let others say. I know but what I know,
And when I know, I have no need to ask.

And as with steps obedient and slow
Homeward I turn, and to the tool-shed go,
With dusk preparing to resume my task,
Take out the shining spade, the trug, the hoe,
Then once more must I stand amazed, for lo
The heavens change, as storm without a sound
Comes from the south, empurpling all the sky
Save where a province of rich gold doth lie
Above the tree-tops, strikes the distant vane,
And sweeps the stubble in a light profound
Such as I never saw, nor hope to see again.

And, fortune piled on fortune, comes a flight
Of snow-white pigeons crossing that dark cloud,
Luminous convoy slow against the wrack;
And as to frame their passage stands a proud
A double rainbow, perfect in its bright
Half-circle touching Heaven, and the ground.

Such things are given; never taken back.

Strange were those summers; summers filled with war.
I think the flowers were the lovelier
For danger. Then we lived the *pundonor*,
Moment of truth and honour, when the bull
Charges and danger is extreme, but skill
And daring over-leap the fallible will
And bring the massive beast to noble kill.
Moments as sharp as sword-points then we lived
Citing our death along the levelled blade;

Then in our petty selves were shaken, sieved,
Withouten leisure left to be afraid.

It was a strange, a fierce, unusual time.
Death's certain threat, that most men think remote,
Not for today, but for another day,
For some tomorrow surely far away,
Unreal as an ancient anecdote,
Came near, and did not smite, but sometimes smote.

We lived exalted to a different clime;
Not in safe seats behind the palisade
Watching while others risk the scarlet sweep
And make the pass of death before the Thing
Cited at bay to take the estocade
And spout the lung-blood dark upon the sand,
Sinking at last in slow and sculptural heap
At foot of the young dazzling matador
Armed only with his sword and wrist and hand,—
Not as spectators in those days of war
But in the stainèd ring.

Strange little tragedies would strike the land;
We sadly smiled, when wrath and strength were spent
Wasted upon the innocent.
Upon the young green wheat that grew for bread;
Upon the gardens where with pretty head
The flowers made their usual summer play;
Upon the lane, and gaped it to a rent
So that the hay-cart could not pass that way.
So disproportionate, so violent,
So great a force a little thing to slay.
—Those craters in the simple fields of Kent!

It took a ton of iron to kill this lark,
*   This weightless freeman of the day.*
All in its fate was irony. It lay
Tiny among monstrosities of clay,
Small solitary victim of the dark.

None other shared its fate, not the soft herd
  Heavily ruminant, full-fed;
Not man or woman in their cottage bed;
Only this small, still-perfect thing lay dead.
I weighed it in my hand. How light, a bird!

Imponderable puff, it should have died
  Singing as it had lived; been found
By death between the heaven and the ground;
Not suffered this eclipse without the sound
Of song by last gross irony denied.

Coppices I have seen, so rudely scarred,
With all their leaves in small confetti strown;
The hazels blasted and the chestnut charred;
Yet by the Autumn, leaves of Spring had grown.
How temporary, War, with all its grief!
Permanence only lay in sap and seed.
They knew that life was all their little need,
And life was still in the untimely leaf.
This was our miniature, our minor share
In Europe's misery and desolation;
Not in our habit; war had never crossed
Our arrogant frontier; others met the cost,
But not our own, our moated isle, our nation.
England was sea-borne, Venus in her shell,
Lovely to her own self, and safe beyond compare;

We had heard echoes of an ernful knell
Sounding across our seas. We were not there.
We were at home, although our sons might go
As young men go, but we at home in slow
Resentment at an insult found at length
That half the sinews of our strength
Were cut by knives that slashed them from the air;
Yet, angry and astonished as we were
We kept our faith and even at moments said

"This war will be over soon."
Yes, in September or perhaps November,
With some full moon or gibbous moon,
A harvest moon or else a hunter's moon
It will be over.

Not for the broken innocent villages,
Not for the broken innocent hearts:
For them it will not be over,
The memorable dread,
The lost home, the lost son, and the lost lover.

Under the rising sun, the waxing moon,
This war will be over soon,
But only for the dead.

Strange were those summer nights, those nights of war.
The sky was all too busy and too full;
Beauty and terror both too bountiful.
We knew not which was which, of sound or sight;
Which held the richer store.
For sound the invisible war-planes overhead
Lost in the star-flecked velvet of the night,
And distant guns that sped
Fountains of fireworks such as children love,
Quick in ascent and languid in descent,
But poised for one pure moment at the peak;
And tracer bullets in a level streak
Cutting below the stars.
                              Then cried that most
Sinister plaint, prophetic sad lament,

Near, and then distant, as the call
Took up in rise and fall,
Ellinge as household ghost;
As beacons once strung out along the Downs,
Took up from villages and little towns
To darkened hamlets in the Weald of Kent
Not safe within the muffle of their oaks;
And from the English coast
Came guns that bruised the door,
Twitched at the windows, quavered in the floor,
And nearer still, and near,
In their great concert came, in thunder-strokes,
And travelled on to London with their roar
Dying away, for other men to hear.

Strange things we did, that none had done before.
Sinister fears beset th' unseasoned mind;
Incalculable science, dubious friend,
More dubious still when turned to evil end;
We saw ourselves in horror choking, blind,
And mad precautions—were they mad or sane?—
Outraged our valid life in a profane
Lunatic twist where guardian science fought
With murderous science, barely to defend
Life which was all, though grace of life was nought.

Strange things indeed, that none had thought to do!
Dug trenches in the orchard when the fruit
Hung for September's picking; hung, and fell
Into the gashes open at the root.
We thrust our children in that clammy cell;
Like beasts we went to earth, for their small sake;
The vixen's litter, hidden in the brake,
Slept softer than the infant sons of men.
And we created darkness. Sons of light
By God's intention, over sea and land
In one wide gesture of erasing hand
We swept that symbol from our natural night.
No window in the sleeping village street,
No window in the cottages discrete;

Hidden, and like a child afraid
Shrinking beneath the bed-clothes that persuade
Into a sense of safety, then
We cowered in our darkness, yet we made
Different light, and watched it from the shades.

So tall and yet so silent as they stride,
Slow scissors walking up and down the black;
Soundless collision of their closing blades
That cut a star in half, and leave no track.
Sound should accompany such giant glide,
Expected sound, to match so grave a scale,
But like all lofty natives of the night
They're mute, it is their very quality.

Only the little native of low glades,
The frog, the owl, the thicket nightingale,
With tiny voice lift sylvan serenades
To different splendour on a different height:
Planets that are, and were not, suddenly
In solitary presence, primrose nail,
Fixed in the wash of sea-green sky as pale;
The dozy moon, the meteor quick in flight,
Are taciturn in their mysterious pride.

So joined in ancient and processional rite
    Comes, unforeseen, this new
Magnificence to take belated place, and slue
    High pivots without sound.
Oh see! their coronet of beams that spear
Our darkness in inverted chandelier
Based on the ordinary ground;
    Notice, the while they veer,
The earth we live on shows both small and round.
We had not known th' horizon thus in curve
Unless at sea. Like truth without a swerve
Stiff from their base they rear their pyramid.
And see, at meeting apex, how they hold
A wide-winged dove, a crucifix in gold.
Is it a dove, soft-feathered? or a plane

Tiny with murder? or a wooden Cross?
   A dove, a plane, a Cross, amid
The meeting beams at their convergent vane?
Here is new beauty turned into our gain.
   This dove, this cross, within the rays
Caught as a floating point across the ways
Of the old skies, their old their travelled floor.
Can beauty then be born of hideous war?
So frightful parent bear so fair a child?
Watching, I wonder; and a hope too wild
Crosses my spirit, to requite our loss.
Can some fine purity emerge from dross,
Washed free from gravel, sifted, ore to find?
If I could not believe so, I must die
And worse than die, give up my soul's belief,
Deep Death beyond the body or the mind,
Grief gone beyond all human thought of grief.

Strange, how these lights examine round our sky . . .

Strangest of all, we knew that it must pass;
We knew the curtained future somewhere held
(However dark the glass,)
That unbelieved-in day of fear expelled
When extraordinary death should cease
And only ordinary death remain,
And men throughout their little world regain
The trim that they call peace.

So in the gardener's more persistent war
Where man not always is the conqueror,
We plodded as we could, and fought
Permanent enemies, of weed and wing:
The strangling bindweed and the running strands
Of crowsfoot, and the suckers of the rose,
Inordinate thorns that mangle our poor hands;
All these must every rank Summer bring,
And August duly brought
Swarms of a summer enemy, of those
Small samurai in lacquered velvet dressed,

Innumerable in their vermin breed
As fierce and fiery as a spark of gleed,
Scavengers on a gormandising quest
To batten on the treasure of our crops
Of promised fruit, our gages, Golden Drops,
Our peaches downy as a youthful cheek,
Our nectarines, in adolescence sleek;
They came, destructive though we sought their nest,
Those fiends that rustic oracles call wopse.

There's not a rhyme to *wasp* in English tongue.
Poor wasp, unloved, unsung!
Only the homely proverb celebrates
These little dragons of the summer day
That each man hates.
'Wasps haunt the honey-pot,' they say,
Or 'Put your hand into a wasps' nest,' thus
Neatly condensing all report for us
By sharp experience into wisdom stung,
As is the proverb's way.

Of many a man it might be said
No one loved him till he was dead,
But of a wasp not even then
As it is said of many men.

Dug by nocturnal badger from his nest;
Branded, as though by his own stripes, a pest;
Every man's hand against him, every dog
Snapping mid-air with fine heraldic leap
Between a summer sleep and summer sleep
On drowsy, drenched, and lotus afternoon
When peaches ripen and the ring-doves croon.

So let me write the wasp his apologue
In blend of hatred, wonder, and of jest;
That moral fable never told
Of little Satan in his black and gold,
His coat of tigerskin;
Fastened, a close, a dreamy glutton lover

Drinking late fig and later nectarine.
Let me discover
Some evil beauty in his striped array,
Bad angel of the wingèd air-borne tribe,
And have the honour of his earliest scribe.

Evil he is; to him was evil given
If evil be within our judgment, when
We seek to sift the purposes of heaven.
Exquisite wasp! that our fine fruit devours,
His taste at least as elegant as ours.
And if he should not strike at meddling men
Why did his Maker arm him with a sting?

He's small, he's vicious, he's an easy prey;
With greater skill our ingenuity
Kills with one crack so intricate a thing;
So difficult to make, beyond our powers.
Man can make man, but there his cunning ends;
That necessary act he can dispatch
As Nature urges, launching out a batch
Of new descendants, rivals, precious friends,
But not an insect subtle on the wing.
Oh Man! now mark:
Could you send out one moth upon the dark,
One bat, one delicate bat, that senses wide
The threads of cotton on his passage tied,
One butterfly with wings ornate
As Byzantine mosaics, flitterling
That in your chimney has the wit to hide
All Winter through, until
With your first sick-room fire, when you are ill
And call for solace of the genial grate,
He with still slothful wings descends
From that dark, sooty gloom
Into the warmth of your close room
To flutter on your window-panes and twitch
The ears of sleepy cur
Happily stretched along your hearth, with bitch
Softly domestic, curved against his fur.

Could you make these? Oh no. But you can kill.

So let me grant the hated wasp his due,
He showed me beauty where I had not thought
Beauty to find. He drove me out with torch
To seek among pale leaves at darkest night
Pale grapes on sculptured porch,
Hanging from column and from architrave
In classical festoon,
Aquamarine, a cave
Of strangest green in that strange light,
And this was beauty. Thanks to him, that knave,
All thanks to him, I sought
The rosy rondure of the moonlit peach
So stilly heavy on her slender twig,
Too often out of reach
So left for him to whom I much forgave;
All thanks to him, I found the Ischian fig
Yellowing in September's yellow moon,
Or Turkey fig burst open to reveal
Mediterranean flesh of Homer's wine-dark sea.
Such nights could indignation much anneal;
I had not seen such fine, such lovely sights
On deeply private nights
But for his mischief in the end my weal.
Much did he take, but more gave back to me.

So stay your hand, your condemnation stay:
Even the wasp, like dog, must have his day,
And as I know that Shakespeare, country lad
Pocketing Venus and Adonis, might
Pocket a Warwick lane, with woodbine, snail,
And turn it all towards a Roman tale
Or else a Belmont and Venetian night,
So do I think that country lad
So English-sane, so universal-mad,
Had wasps in mind, when he of rascal thieves
Wrote, that go suck the subtle blood of the grape.
These were no alien or Athenian thieves;
They were the wasps on plums on Stratford walls.

He stung his fingers, stealing ripened fruit,
No mine or thine,
A schoolboy's loot;
He was a boy, and took his boyish shape
Of mind into his verse, as poets do,
Using small instances to make a line.

And let me end upon a note of hope
For persecuted wasp, so neat, so fine,
That in sarcastic verse I thus enshrine:
It was a wasp that in a glass of wine
Once killed a Pope.

So passes Summer, still without one brief
Respite from labour, simply to enjoy;
Never that empty moment of relief
When every task is done, no urgent ploy.
Martha not Mary bustles to her chares
Living, not saying, her creative prayers.

Save when some cause must interrupt the fret
And force the contemplative blessèd spell
When Martha's garden turns to Mary's cell,
And Martha must her diligence forget.
No cell enclosed, but open to the broad
Vision that knows no wall of time or stone,
When scattered notes resolve into a chord;
The cell where visionary eyes may dwell
On images their own, yet not their own;
Alone, yet less than in companionship alone.

Green vine-shade; sweet airs breathe; leaves lift;
Tendrils in tenderest of shadows drift.
Dog, on the dappled ground your dappled body lay.
Black sun, black humble-bees, black grapes;
Slim carven columns wreathed in vine;
My little world of gently stirring shapes;
Summer, the corn's last standing day.

I'm ill; my body is not mine.

My mind is more than mine, and lifts astray
Up with the leaves, as light as they.
No Thought, but Being; rarest idleness.
Princes, for all I care, may ride away.
I suffer nothing but the air's caress.

Yet in this flute-note shadowed melody
A new companion shares my loneliness:
Some stranger in myself, alone with me.

For our life is terribly private in the end,
In the last resort;
And if our self's a stranger, what's a friend?
A pretty children's game of let's pretend!
We can share nor the puzzle nor the grief,
Neither the physical nor mental pain,
The insecurity, the fears insane . . .
How fortunate, that life should be so brief!

Yet I arise again, and very loth
   Leave that sweet spell of sloth.
Perhaps the better part, to dream and gaze
   And some Creator praise
For bounty that we nothing did to earn,
   And rest content
With green beneath the leaves' translucent tent
   In woods wherein the fern
Uncurls her crozier where the moss is wet
   And the wild violet
Smokes blue along the pack-way in a haze.

All strangely come, with nothing due to man.
   Not his, that perfect plan.
He measures out the stars he could not make,
   He names the sliding snake,
But walks, a witling in the world he owns.
   For all his skill
He fashioned not the Lenten daffodil,
   Nor set between the stones
Gentians by running water in the peat,
   Nor sent the fleet

Of water-lilies sailing on the lake.

His art is imitation, and with love
*   On nature to improve.*
The necessary fool has learnt to see
*   A better model, free*
From labour, lavish in conceit, a wealth
*   Without a fence,*
Plenteous fancy, varied difference,
*   Where he may rob by stealth*
Invention's plunder, since the woods more wise
*   Offer his eyes*
A garden at the foot of every tree.

Now shall the sharpened and well-oilèd shears
Be lifted from their shelf and put to use
On the year's growth of hedges, too profuse.
Order and comeliness must be restored
(Nature the wanton lady, Man the Lord),
As through the weeks the trimmer perseveres,
Leaving with sigh all other jobs for this,
Seeing his borders flounder, seeing new
Weed that, neglected, sportively appears;
But still must drudge on urgent artifice
With aching arms and spine that will not bend
When evening comes, till hedges are abhorred
And stretch in nightmare miles, set end to end.

Whether the twiggy hornbeam or the beech,
The quick, the holly, or the lime to pleach,
Or little box, or gravity of yew
Cut into battlements to frame a view
Before the frost can harm the wounded tips,
Throughout the days he trims and clips and snips,
As must the guardian of the child correct
Distorted growth and tendencies to wrong,
Suppress the weakness, countenance the strong,
Shaping through craft and patience of the years
Into a structure seemly, firm, erect,
Batter and buttress, furious gales to scorn.

He is both gardener and architect
Working in detail on his walls and piers
Of green anatomy, his garden's frame,
Design his object, shapeliness his aim,
Yet, practical, will with big gloves protect
His hands against the blister and the thorn.
Plant not the vulgar privet, to your shame,
Nor laurel far less noble than its name,
Lost to reminder of the Pythian game;
Nor macrocarpa, cheap, and evergreen,
And fast in growth, until some searing day
Of Winter turns it dead and bracken-brown
With nothing left to do but cut it down,
That cypress wrongly called of Monterey.
How wrongly! I have seen
At Monterey where sand is silver-clean
And the Pacific azure to Cathay
And nothing passes but a passing ship,
That different tree upon its moon-white strand,
Twisted and dark, alone with sea and sand.
Strange coast, strange tree upon its chosen strip
Of the available world, this edge of land.

Not only on those narrow miles apart
It grows, but travels in the stricken heart
Of those who learnt its beauty in a brief
Vision, and kept it as a constant fief.

Plant box for edging; do not heed the glum
Advice of those unthinking orthodox
Gardeners who condemn the tidy box
As haven for the slug, through winter numb.
Slugs will find shelter, box or nany box,
Therefore plant straightly, and with August come
Clip neatly (you may also clip in May
If time allow, a double yearly trim
To make your edging thicker and more prim,)
And in the scent of box on genial day
When sun is warm as seldom in this isle,
Smell something of the South, as clippings pile

Beneath your tread, like aromatic spray
Strewn down the paving of cathedral aisle
On pagan-Christian feast-day, for the feet
Of the devout to crush, who know not what they do
Save that they breathe an air both sharp and sweet.

Or as in some old hall, where dogs abound,
Sniffing for bones across the littered ground,
Herbs pungent mixed with wood-smoke and with peat,
The rosemary, the tansy, and the rue.

So for your garden choose the lavish best;
Impatience and a false economy
Never made value yet, so gravely plant
Even the slowest and the costliest
And wait for the reward the years will grant.
Consider those who, selfless, placidly
Thought for the future and themselves endured
Vistas of sticks, absurd, in formal line,
That should be leafy avenues, matured.
Le Nôtre saw a skeleton design,
Content if but the future were assured.

Aristocrat of hedges, noble yew!
Our English cypress, feudal, stately, dark,
Nurtured on blood of bullocks, patriarch,
Whether in venerable avenue
Or single on the road, a pilgrim's mark.
Ancestral yew! yet fain to fantasy,
Lending its dignity
To such caprice as takes the gardener's mind,
In topiary elaborate
Of Pliny's Tuscan villa, or the state
Of royal palace and of country-seat,
Tortured to such conceit
As chessmen, dragons, elephants resigned
To carry howdahs; obelisk most neat,
Pyramids mocking Egypt, cannon-balls
For ever static on their verdant walls;
Or crownèd queen upon an arm-chair throne;

No natural growth, but vaunted specimen,
Ingenious and laborious feat
Of many slavish gardeners of rich men
That thus through years the patient yew maltreat.

Only, an echo at the cottage-gate
In simple drollery diverts the hind.
He nothing knows of Pliny, nor what great
Topiary tradition lies behind.
He only knows that when his work is done
For others, and he turns towards his own,
He will indulge his serious sense of fun;
Will train a pheasant sitting on her eggs,
A homely kettle, with a proper spout;
The things he knows: a stool on three thin legs;
A pig, a silent pig, in dark dark green,
Such as in pigstye never yet was seen;
And as his children watch and prance and shout
"Father! make grow a ring within his snout,"
He grins, and ably twists some wire and twine
To turn his pig into a porcupine.
Soon will his pheasant fly from off her nest,
His kettle pour. . . . He jests. I also jest.

But yew, that prince, that poet of our trees
That to our humour docile condescends
And in fantastic shapes both twists and leans,
(As Shakespeare gave the groundlings comic scenes
Of clowns and knock-about,
And would not scorn to please
His simple countrymen, his lowly friends,
Yet carried them in magic and alarm
Into unearthly regions, to draw breath
So rarified, they wondered what was near,
What strange suggestion, what strange hand and arm
Reached out to touch them from the haunts of fear,
What cipher written in what shibboleth,
What depths of shadow, chasms of the soul,
Translated on to variegated scroll
Now wise, now mad, now colourless, now gay,

All life, and that beyond, which we call death,)
So does the yew, the architectural yew,
In sombre mood or freakish match our day.
By moonlight it but tells us what we knew,
That all is tenebrous, uncertain, lit
In fitful patches mingled with the gloom
More beautiful because indefinite:
The chamber of the day or of the tomb?
The moonlight falls deceptive: who can say?

Yet the strong daylight makes the yew a grove,
A very temple of retreat or love,
Suggestive shadows richly ambient.
Then will such arbours charm the musing mind,
Or stone-flagged path, significantly straight,
The pacing footstep, as, with head inclined,
The scholar, the philosopher, the lover,
In endless up-and-down may strictly rove,
Patrolling sentry thinking out his fate,
And some new regulated truth discover,
Some allegorical solution find
In geometrical restriction held;
Passions enclosed, their bursting nature pent
Between the calming linear walls confined,
Gently rebuked and tolerantly quelled.

This is the tranquil, ancient, wise, sedate
Counsellor yew, not briskly eloquent
But, to the listener, with much to say;
As much as glades that whisper in a wood
But neater and more orderly than they.
But if in lighter mood
You would plant hedges, think upon the gay
Frivolous boundaries that toss their spray
In colour on beholden air.
Seemingly wild, yet not too wild, too rough;
An art in wildness, even in the bluff
And thorny branches of the hedgerow May,
Red, rose, or white; or in the cloudy puff
Of ceanothus, blue and powdery;

Or hedge of roses, growing devil-care,
—Rose of the World; th' embroidered Tuscany;
The scented Cabbage, and the Damascene;
Sweet-briar, lovelier named the eglantine;
But above all the Musk
With classic names, Thisbe, Penelope,
Whose nectarous load grows heavier with the dusk
And like a grape too sweetly muscadine.

So let invention riot. Dare
Th' unorthodox; be always bold; be prince;
This is your realm; let fancy flaunt and flare;
Fail if you must, outrageous heretic,
But gloriously fail: the dream, the brag,
No prudent prose, but lyric rhetoric.

So for your headges plant the tossing quince,
Cydonia many-coloured as a flag,
In sentimental Apple-Bloom, full-blown,
Or Knaphill Scarlet, wrongly named, that rag
Coral not scarlet, flown
Startling against a sky as gray as stone;
Or, deep as a Venetian robe outspread
Against a cottage wall, the veteran Red.

Or plant in jewelled swagger, twin with use,
Myrobolans, prolific cherry-plum,
Topaz and ruby, where the bees may hum
In early blossom, and, with Summer come,
Children and wasps dispute the wealth of juice.
Level your hedge by pruning to the spur,
But here and there, at intervals designed,
Let a strong tree go up in loftier
Canopy hung with fruit, a spreading cry,
As from the tedious level of mankind
Once in a generation rise the high
Lanterns of the imaginative mind.
And since the garden's backbone is the Hedge
Shaping to seemly order, set it square,
Not in weak curves that half deny the pledge

Given to pattern in intent austere.
Gardens should be romantic, but severe.
Strike your strong lines, and take no further care
Of such extravagance as pours the rose
In wind-blown fountains down the broken walls,
In gouts of blood, in dripping flower-falls,
Or flings the jasmine where the walls enclose
Separate garths, a miniature surprise.
Marry excess to an adroit repose,
With no confusion of a plan so clear
It speaks its outline to the mind and eyes,
Instant, intelligible, and sincere,
As should be, seldom is, the life of man.

And set the axis of your garden plan
In generous vistas reaching to a bourn
Far off, yet visible, a certain term
Definite as ambition, and as firm;
Stopped by a statue or a little urn
Cut to contain the ashes of a stern
Roman (the ruin of his villa lies
Buried beneath the barley, near our coast.)

That small sarcophagus, that nameless shrine
Set in a square-cut niche of yew, alone,
So shadowy it breeds the curly fern,
Shall speak for the male Roman, dead but strong,
The salutary necessary ghost.
Let the nymph stand for beauty's token sign,
Slanting her head beneath her wreath of stone,
About to clash her cymbals, always mute;
With elbow crook'd and one suggestive hand
Ready to drop towards her loosened zone;
Glancing towards the Roman, wistfully,
As ever in a profitless pursuit
Beauty shall beckon to mortality.

And these shall be your symbols; let them stand
Looking at one another down the long
Grave path you planned as not your life you planned.

But if so rarely fortunate you be
That God runs water through your English home,
River or brook, or little pricking spring,
Remember how the fountains play in Rome.
Enforce the most from this most living thing.
The lark has not a finer, sweeter song
Than drips of water, orient as pearl,
In moon-laid ovals dropped upon a rock
Splashing through night and day, eternally,
Regular as the ticking of a clock
But with a loveliness no clock of time
Might ever tell, or quarters ever chime.

And if your river yet more wildly swirl
Set your quiescent nymph beside it; dip
Her foot within the water; let her look
Across the separation of the brook
Towards her soldier where the ferns unfold
In green that later turns to bracken-gold;
Even as on her nape the pearl and curl
Cluster against the bending of her head
So virginal, so tender, and so sweet
It seems a lover's kiss must falter there
Amongst the tendrils of her volute hair
In subtler kiss than kiss on parting lip;

Yet by their nature they may never meet
Since she is marble, and her soldier dead.

Water is living; water springs from earth,
Whether from mountains poured in melting stream
Or risen in the stones, a bubbling birth
Struck by some Moses from a sombre dream,
Some Pisgah vision, some divining-rod
That finds in rock the hidden hint of God.
Water is living; water tells its tale,
Its legendary music; coots and swans
Swim to the summons in their various plume,
Olive as water glossy in the gloom,
Blue-white as sumptuous as mountains snows

Sun-smitten where the sources first arose,
—The high land paramount, the low land paravail,—
And circle at that bidding, dark or pale,
Around the pool, explore the little creek,
And delicately drink with dipping beak
The silver water from the urn of bronze.

AUTUMN

AUTUMN in felted slipper shuffles on,
Muted yet fiery,—Autumn's character.
Brown as a monk yet flaring as a whore,
And in the distance blue as Raphael's robe
Tender around the Virgin.

                Blue the smoke
Drifting across brown woods; but in the garden
Maples are garish, and surprising leaves
Make sudden fires with sudden crests of flame
Where the sun hits them; in the deep-cut leaf
Of peony, like a mediaeval axe
Of rusty iron; fervour of azalea
Whose dying days repeat her June of flower;
In Sargent's cherry, upright as a torch
Till ravelled sideways by the wind to stream
Disorderly, and strew the mint of sparks
In coins of pointed metal, cooling down;
And that true child of Fall, whose morbid fruit
Ripens, with walnuts, only in November,

The Medlar lying brown across the thatch;
Rough elbows of rough branches, russet fruit
So blet it's worth no more than sleepy pear,
But in its motley pink and yellow leaf
A harlequin that some may overlook
Nor ever think to break and set within
A vase of bronze against a wall of oak,
With Red-hot Poker, Autumn's final torch.

The medlar and the quince's globe of gold.
How rich and fat those yellow fruits do hang!
They were light blossom once, a light-foot girl,
All cream and muslin once, now turned to age
Mellow with fine experience. The sun
Burnt in one season what the years must need
For a girl's ripening. He was the lover
In dilatory half-awakened Spring;
He was the husband of the fruitful Summer,
Father of pregnancy that brings those fruits
Ready to drop at the first touch of hand
Carefully lifting at the parting stalk,
Or at the first wild breath of wind, so soft
You think it harmless, till it blows the vanes
Crooked this way and that, a treacherous wind
Bringing the apples down before their date.

All's brown and red: the robin and the clods,
And umber half-light of the potting-shed,
The terra-cotta of the pots, the brown
Sacking with its peculiar autumn smell,
Musty in corners, where the cobweb panes
Filter the sun, to bronze the patient heaps
Of leaf-mould, loam, and tan of wholesome peat;
And sieves that orderly against the wall
Dangle from nail, with all the panoply
(Brightened by oily rag) of shining tools,
The gardener's armour, pewter as a lake,
And good brown wood in handles and in shafts;
Plump onion and thin bassen raffia
Slung from the rafters where the ladders prop.

And in the gloom, with his slow gesture, moves
The leathern demiurge of this domain,
Like an old minor god in corduroy
Setting and picking up the things he needs,
Deliberate as though all Time were his.
Honour the gardener! that patient man
Who from his schooldays follows up his calling,
Starting so modestly, a little boy
Red-nosed, red-fingered, doing what he's told,
Not knowing what he does or why he does it,
Having no concept of the larger plan.
But gradually, (if the love be there,
Irrational as any passion, strong,)
Enlarging vision slowly turns the key
And swings the door wide open on the long
Vistas of true significance. No more
Is toil a vacant drudgery, when purport
Attends each small and conscientious task,
—As the stone-mason setting yard by yard
Each stone in place, exalting not his gaze
To measure growth of structure or assess
That slow accomplishment, but in the end
Tops the last finial and, stepping back
To wipe the grit for the last time from eyes,
Sees that he built a temple,—so the true
Born gardener toils with love that is not toil
In detailed time of minutes, hours, and days,
Months, years, a life of doing each thing well;
The Life-line in his hand not rubbed away
As you might think, by constant scrape and rasp,
But deepened rather, as the line of Fate,
By earth imbedded in his wrinkled palm;
A golden ring worn thin upon his finger,
A signet ring, no ring of human marriage,
On that brown hand, dry as a crust of bread,
A ring that in its circle belts him close
To earthly seasons, and in its slow thinning
Wears out its life with his.
That hand, that broke with tenderness and strength
Clumps of the primrose and the primula,

Watched by a loving woman who desired
Such tenderness and strength to hold her close,
And take her passionate giving, as he held
His broken plants and set them in the ground,
New children; but he had no thought of her.
She only stood and watched his capable hand
Brown with the earth and golden with the ring,
And knew her part was small in his lone heart.

So comes he at the last to that long Paradise
Where grateful Pharaoh hews a mountain tomb
For the good gardener, the faithful slave,
(Slave not of royalty, but his own piety,)
Painting the vaulted roof of that deep cave
With fresco of imperishable fruit
Such as no earthly gardener ever grew,
Pale peaches and pale grapes, so healthy-heavy
Yet slung from tendrils of a filament
Too weak to bear a locust's weight. He sleeps,
No pest, no canker troubling that deep sleep,
Under the pattern that he scarce divined.

Such gardeners we have known. We cannot cut
Sepulchres in the mountains, on a butt
Of stone within the Valley of the Kings
In the perennial sunshine of the Nile
To do them honour. Such extravagant things
Are not within the scope of our cheap style.
To do them honour we can only give
On paper, not papyrus, not on rock
Graven, the simplest words in epitaph
To make their courage and their memory live.
So will I write for one fine gardener
Who died too young, caught up in folly's flock,
This epitaph of gratitude, in grief
That he, who so loved life, found life so brief.

He had the love of plants, the eager eyes,
The tender fingers, and the neatest skill.
English, he told me how he longed to see

Our garden flowers on their native hill
Before he died. He thought that life was long . . .

Now he has seen them, as in flames he fell
Downwards towards the steep Illyrian cleft
And caught their colour lit by flames of Hell.

God grant, he never thought his fate was wrong;
God grant, he had a vision of the gift
Of his desire, by danger sanctified;
God grant, he saw in one last moment's rift
That carpet spread beneath him as he died.

Move onward, Life; we cannot stop to grieve.
The seed demands the soil, that it may live;
This mystery of contact, strange, devout
In union, as the general scheme of love.
See, in our careful hoard of leaf-mould, sprout
Chestnuts from conkers, little pallid leaf
Of beech from mast, from acorn little oak,
Each in their germination hopefully
Intent on growing to a forest tree;
Close consequence that seed and soil provoke!
Each to his kind, majestic or minute,
Following unaware but resolute
The pre-ordainèd plan
That makes an oak, a daisy, or a man.

So at the potting-bench we play the part
Of gods, and at our humour give
Life's opportunity as we decree.
Flattering power! when our studied art
Dragoons unruly Nature to our hand.
Toss infant oaks aside, and through the sieve
Pass virgin loam and leaf-mould, mixed with sand,
Open and sharp and rich, where seedlings start
Astonished into life, and safely stand
The winter through; or in the open drill
Sow hardier seeds, that from the Winter's ill
Grow more robust and ready for the sweet
Lenience of the Spring when days expand;

179

As the poor orphan that the Fates maltreat
Toughens uncoddled in the frost, the sleet,
Expecting nothing else from world unkind
Where he who lives not, dies;
But at the first soft touch awakes to throw
Blossoms of thankfulness in wild surprise
Such different aspect of the world to find,
And in the kiss of sun forgets the snow.

So Autumn's not the end, not the last rung
Of any ladder in the yearly climb,
When that is deathly old which once was young,
Since time's no ladder but a constant wheel
Like an old paddled mill that dips and churns
The mill-race, and upon the summit turns
Unceasingly to heel
Over, and scoop fresh water out of time.

Autumn's a preparation for renewal,
Yet not entirely shorn
Of tardy beauty, last and saddest jewel
Bedizening where it may not adorn.
Few of the autumn blooms are deeply dear,
Lacking the spirit volatile and chaste
That blows across the ground when pied appear
The midget sweets of Spring, and in their haste
The vaporous trees break blossom pale and clear,
—Carpet and canopy, together born.

Stalwarts of Autumn lack that quality;
Only the little frightened cyclamen
With leveret ears laid back look fresh and young,
Or those pure chalices that Kentish men
Call Naked Boys, but by a lovelier name
Others call Naked Ladies, slender, bare,
Dressed only in their amethystine flame,
The Meadow Saffron magically sprung
By dawn in morning orchards in the grass
Near paths where shepherds on their errand pass
But ender-night beheld no crocus-colour there.

These in the sodden season (unaware
That in their fragile temper they belong
Rightly to Spring and to the early song
Of birds that in September's April days
Bring music back to fill the empty air
And knot the fugue into the final phrase
Repetitive, and with a looping thong
Coil round our hearts prepared to weep
Their valedictory tears
Over the irrecoverable years,
Over lost youth, lost hope, and that fine leap
Vaulting all obstacle of doubts and fears,
Strong, confident, excited, and inspired
By youth's divine unwisdom, never tired
And never longing for the final sleep,)
These in their sudden springing and their youth
Restore the ecstasy that once we took for truth.

So in September when a day of rain
Holds up your outdoor work, make gain
Out of your seeming loss; devote
A morning to those bleaker days remote
Of January through to March as bleak
When flow'rs are few to find and cold to seek,
(The hellebore, bespattered with the mud;
The daring primrose meek
Hiding beside the little brook in flood
Come long before her time;
The winter aconite that gilds the rime
Between the spillikins of grass;
The jasmine sprays that in a fountain fall,)
These with cold fingers picked and brought
Under the lamplight in a pool of small
Surprising colour, tabled in a glass,
Dearer because so difficultly sought,
Miniature triumphs rescued from the storm,
—These shall be supplemented by your thought
Prophetic, while September yet is warm.

Pack the dark fibre in the potter's bowl;

Set bulbs of hyacinth and daffodil,
Jonquil and crocus, (bulbs both sound and whole,)
Narcissus and the blue Siberian squill.
Set close, but not so tight
That flow'ring heads collide as months fulfil
Their purpose, and in generous sheaf expand
Obedient to th' arrangement of your hand.
Yours is the forethought, yours the sage control.

Keep the too eager bulbs from ardent light;
Store in a gloomy cupboard, not too chill;
Give grateful moisture to the roots unseen,
And wait until the nose of bleachèd shoot
Pushes its inches up, in evidence
That many worms of root
Writhe whitely down to fill
The darkness of the compost, tangled, dense.
Then may you set your bowls on window sill
And smile to see the pallor turn to green.
Fat, pregnant, solid horns, that overnight
Swell into buds, and overnight again
Explode in colour, morning's sudden stain,
In long succession, nicely planned between
Epiphany and Easter, if so be
Easter falls early and the window-pane
Still shows the fine the crisp anatomy
Of fern-like frosted frond,
And nothing in the waiting soil beyond.

But in October, later, shall you stand
With paper sack of bulbs and plunge your hand
And careless fling your bulbs both large and small
To roll, to topple, settling sparse or thick,
Over the grass, and plant them where they fall,
(Legitimate device, a sanctioned trick.)
Thus in a drift as though by Nature planned
Snowdrops shall blow in spreading tide,
Little white horses breaking on the strand
At edge of orchard; and the orange-eyed
Narcissus of the poets in a wide

AUTUMN

Lyrical river flowing as you pass
Meandering along the path of grass.

Their names are little poems in themselves:
Grand Soleil d'Or, great golden sun,
Earliest in its gift, with Winter Gold.
Their very names are Light, when days are dun.
Seagull, and Sunrise,—are they sailing-ships?
What Golden Spur pricked Fortune and Desire?
What Queen of Spain was loved by Sweet Adare?
What Emperor kissed Roxana on the lips?

Yet Autumn calls for courage, as the end
Of all things calls for courage,—love or life;
Seldom with clean-cut slicing of the knife,
But a slow petering, a dismal droop,
As browning asters tied into a group
No lovelier than a birch-broom, in a head
Soggy, and dank, and very nearly dead.
Then in such days the flame of faith is low;
Spring is far off, and in the Winter dread
Most tepidly and cowardly we go.

My mood is like a fire that will not heat;
There's touchwood, and a chequer-board of peat;
The sturdy logs laid ready, sere and dry;
The match-box, and the chimney swept and high;
There's all the setting for a roar of flame
But love and poetry are but a name,
And neither will my fuel burn, nor I.

Flame of my hearth, a grizzled heap of ash;
Flame of my heart, turned trumpery and trash.
Did I live once? did once my timber flare?
Did I dare all that now I do not dare?
Did once I kindle, leap, lick high, scorch, blaze,
In splendid arson of my reckless days?
I, smothered clinker, cold and un-aware?

Get hence, damp mood, as musty as the shroud,
Such sulky torpor suits no spirit proud;

183

Come, flame; come, tongue of courage; scorch me, sear;
I'll risk the burning to regain the clear
Fangs of returning life as sharp as fire.
Better, I swear, to be consumed entire
Than smoulder, knowing neither zest nor fear.

Then, in a sudden spurt revived, I cry
As both my mood and litten fire burn high,

Oh Days, be double! Hours, be forty-eight!
Oh Time, be rathe for once, instead of late!
Oh Sun, stand still! Oh Moon, neglect to rise!
Oh Daylight, dilly-dally in the skies!

Oh life too rich, oh years too fleet, too fleet,
Oh simple thought, that going youth is sweet!
Was never felt such truth-in-platitude
Till rapid rush of our incertitude.

Not the white hairs, but oh the end, the end!
The little that we know, the love, the friend,
The room, the garden path, the day's affairs,
The movements of the heart, the joys, despairs.

Oh bolting Time, rough pony of my days,
Halt by the hedgerow of my life to graze.
Halt but an hour; there's pulse as strong as mine,
There's herbage still, there's ramage, vetch, and bine.

Halt, and consider as you wildly go:
I am the only thing I truly know,
My extant life my only episode;
Your rattling course completes my only road,

The only chapter of my narrative.
My verb is still in the indicative.
Oh years gone by! oh years still going past
In wild crescendo, fast and ever fast
Like some mad back-cloth scenes that, worked
     at speed,
Drawn backwards in their prospect still recede,
And I, oh God! not ready yet to live.

Now the dark yew, that sombre secret soul,
Bears fruit, more coral than our ugly blood;
Bright wax within the green, a tallow stud
Most exquisite in substance and in form,
Strewn by the birds and by the soft wild storm
In sprinkled carpet underneath the bays
Of taxine carpentry, these autumn days.

The breeze that autumn night was hot and south.
I met a frog that carried in his mouth
One of those berries, on unknown intent.
So brisk, so earnest, in his ranine hurry,
I stood aside to let him take his bent.
He had his right to's life as I to mine;
I had my right to my descriptive line,
He had his right to his more precious berry.
I stopped, he hopped, I watched him where he went.
He had no fear of me and could not doubt
What love I had for him, that blebbed and queer
Visitant from the woodland mere
Who, gaudy with his berry sticking out,

Met me beneath the cavern of the porch
As we were meant to meet,
—Miniature monster circled at my feet
Within the coin of my miraculous torch.

He lowly, and the architectural porch so tall,
But he, in *his* way, also a miracle.

Gone in the morning, but nocturnal yew
Bore evidence of writing in the night,
Somnambulistic poems, fine and light,
Glistering webs down the long avenue,
Hammocks of fancy, geometric maze,
A spell that never might a poet write.
These mushroom days, these moist and misty days
When the drenched grass looks heavy with the dew
And all the distance shrouded into shapes
Dimly divined, the ghost of what we knew,
Solid with apples hanging in the haze,
Red as a smaller sun, and nearer to our gaze;
And on the rosy walls the greening grapes
And pears already sleepy with their weight.
Brambles turn black, the little sloe turns blue,
Dark in the heraldry of Autumn's state,
And by high undern staring in amaze
We cry "The sun has come through! the sun is through!"

There reigns a rusty richness everywhere;
See the last orange roses, how they blow
Deeper and heavier than in their prime,
In one defiant flame before they go;
See the red-yellow vine leaves, how they climb
In desperate tangle to the upper air;
So might a hoyden gipsy toss and throw
A scarf across her disobedient hair.
See the last zinnias, waiting for the frost,
The deadly touch, the crystals and the rime,
Intense of colour, violent, extreme,
Loud as a trumpet lest a note be lost
In blackened death that nothing can redeem;

They make the most of moments that remain,
And with the florid dahlia, ruddy stain,
Endorse the sun-clock's motto, sour and plain:
THE WHOLE OF LIFE IS BUT A POINT OF TIME.
See the red dogwood, lacquered by the rain.
That's tough, that's savage, that will stand the strong
Usage of Winter till the Spring again
Clothe with less lovely leaf its Indian vein.
But through the days too short and nights too long
Slow damage works, as age upon our span,
Damping or withering the clumps of green,
Wet bundles now of sad and sodden tan.
How tall they were, how quick of growth, how keen,
How bravely they began,
How bravely met the full meridian
Challenge of high young life, that now are brown,
Dirty with waning bindweed and with vetch
At year's end as at last we cut them down,
Playing the part of death, that soon ourselves will fetch.

(Yet, for a moment, in these dying days,
St. Luke will bring his little Summer, when
Faith may restore the tired hearts of men,
Ready to doubt but readier to believe.
Oh sweet St. Luke, so happy to deceive!
Evangelist, he brushes with his pen
A golden light in strokes of golden rays
From Heaven fanning down upon the maize
Strewn through the dust-motes to the pheasants, in
The orchard where the yaffle and the jays
Streak a bright feather as they take to wing.
And as in February hints of Spring
Cozen us into courage, so this late
Golden revival, in a last reprieve,
May stay the hour to wait,
As in the shadows Death
Slides back the moving sword within the sheath.)

The faded spinster, soft in gray,
Bends to the old romantic stone;

She reads the words that kindly say
'The heart not always lived alone.'
Set in her flowers of today
The dial speaks of other flowers
When she was prettier than they,
And laughed at shadows and at showers,
Knowing that sun succeeded rain,
Being in love, and loved again,
(That rare return of mortal gift,
That rare, sweet closure of the rift
When 'me and mine' is 'us and ours'.)
I NUMBER NONE BUT SUNNY HOURS.

She loves the motto with its dear
Suggestion that all things are well;
Within her heart it rings a clear
Tinkle of sentimental bell.
Others may heed the voice of fear,
The wild beast lurking in the lair,
The heads that frightful may appear
In floating masks upon the air;
But not for her the line that saith
ONE HOUR WILL BE THE HOUR OF DEATH;
The graven words, too true, too plain,
Too fraught with an alarm insane,
And not for her the line too bare
That saith OF THE LAST HOUR BEWARE.

BRIGHT SOL AND LUNA TIME AND TIDE DOTH HOLD;
Bright Sol doth shine the dial with his gold,
But the companion pencil slews a line
In tortoise-travel, fatal, and so fine
No thicker than a hair, a stroke of ink:
IT IS ALREADY LATER THAN YOU THINK.

THE SHADOW TEACHES, better than the light;
The pilgrim hours go by, as thread by thread
The moving pointer eats our little day
Till it be eaten nearly all away
And nothing left us but the final shred.

AND HOW WE GO MAY SHADOW SHOW.
SOONER OR LATER ALL MUST GO.

Then comes reprieving night, forgetful sleep.
Surely the gnomon's shadow cannot creep
Across the dial in a dark so deep?
Oh pitiable man, you have forgot the moon.
What of the moon, that spectral sun of night,
White shepherd of the tides and folded sheep?
She is your orb of night-time, that may sweep
Her midnight shadow as the shade of noon.
You are not safe, by noon-day or by night;
Light's dangerous, no safety is in light;
Dark's dangerous, no safety is in night;
No safety there, since the prescriptive moon
Of lovers cuts our moments into slice
Even in most romantic nights of June,
And measures them in minutes too precise.

She marks our passage, even as the sun,
And in the waste of sleep our life is half-way done.
So does the shadow of the cypress veer
On terraces that meet the trysting moon;
Great lawns or water, raven looking-glass,
Shot-silk of crawling black and malachite
Level and deep and dark.
The liquid or the verdurous lagoon
Deserted register the moving mark,
The silent blade that scythes far more than grass,
Noiseless, remorseless, and too cold to sear.
Tenebrous transit, thieving hour and year
The while we sleep, as though we were not here.
Only the statue, mossed in ancient green,
Eternal in her marble, sure, serene,
Watches, or does not watch, with calm surmise
Events that she has seen, or has not seen,
Passing before her blind indifferent eyes.

Low sinks the sun, and long the shadows fall.
The sun-clock, faithful measurer of time,

Fixed to man's dwelling on his flimsy wall
Or tabled flat on curving pedestal
Amongst his dying flowers, tells the last
Hours of the year as to a funeral,
With silent music, solemn and sublime.
Now is the sunlight ebbing, faint and fast
In intermittent gleams that seldom cut
Throughout the day the quadrant of our fate
With the slow stroke that says TOO SOON . . . TOO LATE . .
The stroke that turns our present to our past.
BEWARE, THE OPEN GATE WILL SOON BE SHUT.

November sun that latens with our age,
Filching the zest from our young pilgrimage,
Writing old wisdom on our virgin page.
Not the hot ardour of the Summer's height,
Not the sharp-minted coinage of the Spring
When all was but a delicate delight
And all took wing and all the bells did ring;
Not the spare Winter, clothed in black and white,
Forcing us into fancy's eremite,
But gliding Time that slid us into gold
Richer and deeper as we grew more old
And saw some meaning in this dying day;
Travellers of the year, who faintly say
How could such beauty walk the common way?